Praise for THE PROTECTOR

"Mary Beth's memoir highlights the challenges she faced as a woman in the testosterone-filled field of security and is a must-read for any woman working in a man's world. I would trust her to protect my six anytime."

—SUE ANN BAKER, FORMER US SECRET SERVICE AGENT, AUTHOR OF *BEHIND THE SHADES*

"This book succeeds on two levels: it's a gripping account of one agent's storied career protecting presidents, CEOs, and heiresses from harm. And it's also a lesson in what it takes to excel as a woman in a hypermasculine world, where you can never, ever let down your guard."

—AMANDA RIPLEY, AUTHOR OF *THE UNTHINKABLE: WHO SURVIVES WHEN DISASTER STRIKES—AND WHY*

"Mary Beth epitomizes the old saying 'When one door closes, another door opens.' Beginning with her FBI and Secret Service experiences, disappointed but undeterred, she never looked back, always pursuing the next opportunity, the next challenge. Her book is a testimony to her fearless approach to her life and to the future. We can all learn from her journey and accomplishments. An honest, humorous, and insightful rendering of life in the world of a Secret Service and personal security agent."

—RALPH BASHAM, FORMER DIRECTOR, UNITED STATES SECRET SERVICE

"A very entertaining read. Mary Beth provides a candid, heartfelt inside look at the joys and frustrations of a career spent protecting others."

—BILL PRIESTAP, FELLOW, GEORGETOWN UNIVERSITY WALSH SCHOOL OF FOREIGN SERVICE, AND FORMER HEAD OF THE FBI COUNTERINTELLIGENCE DIVISION

"*The Protector* is a guide for those many times when you need to reach deep down for the power, energy, and endurance to survive life's difficult times."

—DR. MAURICE PROUT, CLINICAL PSYCHOLOGIST

"Dr. Mary Beth Janke shows us in *The Protector* her courage and perseverance as she pushes toward her goal. She allows the reader a view into her mind and soul as she matures and ultimately finds what she is destined to do."

—ANNA RAIMONDI, AUTHOR OF *CONVERSATIONS WITH MARY*

The
PROTECTOR

MARY BETH WILKAS JANKE

THE

PROTECTOR

A Woman's Journey from the Secret Service to Guarding VIPs and Working in Some of the World's Most Dangerous Places

*The Protector: A Woman's Journey from the
Secret Service to Guarding VIPs and Working
in Some of the World's Most Dangerous Places*

© 2020 Mary Beth Wilkas Janke

Published by
Mary Beth Wilkas Janke
marybethwilkas.com

Hardcover ISBN: 978-1-7346671-2-7
Paperback ISBN: 978-1-7346671-0-3
Ebook ISBN: 978-1-7346671-1-0

Cover and interior design by
Chad W. Beckerman: chadwbeckerman.com
Editing and production by
Reading List Editorial: readinglisteditorial.com

Some of the names in this memoir
have been changed for security
and other reasons.

TO MY PARENTS

Who supported me through
life and throughout my career, even
though it wasn't always easy, and who
taught me to do what's right, even
though doing the right thing doesn't
always lead to a favorable outcome.

AND TO MY HUSBAND

For his sage advice and perspective
throughout this process, for his
unwavering belief in my personal
story, and for his sincere
encouragement as I traveled
down another long,
winding road.

FOREWORD

The Protector chronicles Mary Beth's career path, which begins in 1990 with the United States Secret Service. Thirty years later, she's a university professor with a doctorate in Clinical Psychology. As it is often said, "It's not the destination—it's the journey," and the journey from Agent Wilkas to Dr. Wilkas has certainly been full of surprises.

At times the journey was an uphill battle. *The Protector* is about overcoming the kind of adversity that would have ended most careers—but instead, Mary Beth rises to the occasion to become one of the best and most sought-after protectors in the profession.

Throughout the book, her actions and reactions exhibited the ethics and morals that were instilled in her by her parents. These valuable life lessons learned from her parents guided her through adversity. Through her work ethic and a belief that "well done is better than well said," she gained the respect of all those she worked with, including those she protected, and in the process created a career that few, if any, male or female, have or will ever achieve.

It is the only book I have read that chronicles the other side of the equation—the feelings of those who are being protected, those who need Mary Beth to keep their children from harm. She explains the thoughts of the superwealthy as they experience threats to themselves and their families—and what she did to ease their fears. Those chapters of *The Protector* read like a novel.

Although not intended to be a protective services training manual, *The Protector* supplies more educational content than most books that are meant to be training manuals. This memoir offers a roadmap to success for those working in the protection profession at any level of skill or experience.

The Protector is not only for those in the security and protection profession. Mary Beth's inspirational memoir also applies to people from all walks of life and working in all professions, and I am privileged to have witnessed the incredible journey of Agent Wilkas to Dr. Wilkas.

TONY SCOTTI
CEO, SCOTTI SCHOOL, TONY SCOTTI ASSOCIATES; FOUNDER, INTERNATIONAL SECURITY DRIVER ASSOCIATION

PROLOGUE

"Wilkas, the boss is on the phone." My supervisor's voice cut through the cold morning to where I was huddled in the driveway with my colleagues. We were discussing how to divvy up the day's duties protecting Marshall and Walker Bush, the young grandchildren of President George H. W. Bush who lived at the house we were standing outside of.

"Ha, ha. Yeah, right." At first, I thought he was joking. In my year with the Secret Service, I had never received a phone call in the field. After all, it was the early nineties, the Dark Ages of technology by today's standards, and hardly anyone had a cell phone, let alone one that fit in the palm of the hand.

"Listen, Special Agent in Charge Basham wants to talk to you." My supervisor was stone-faced. He most definitely wasn't pulling my leg. "The phone is on the front seat of my car."

I tugged my coat tighter around me. It had barely cracked thirty degrees that morning. As a native of Chicago, I was no stranger to frosty winters, but for reasons I wouldn't fully understand until later, my supervisor's words sent a chill up my spine. When the Special Agent in Charge (SAIC) of the Washington Field Office of the US Secret Service (USSS) wanted to talk to you, it usually meant one of two things: either there was a problem with a case you were working, or there was a problem with you. As I jogged toward my supervisor's car, my mind reached for other explanations.

Think positive, I reminded myself. *Maybe you're actually going to be allowed to move into the counterfeit squad way earlier than anticipated.*

I knew it would be almost unheard of for someone as new as I was to the Secret Service to be moved out of the check forgery squad so quickly, but I fantasized nonetheless, desperate to alleviate the sinking feeling in my stomach. It wouldn't be the craziest thing, I reasoned. I got along well with pretty much everyone on the job, from fellow agents to supervisors, all the way up to the bosses. Even though I was in the minority as a woman, I was well liked, as far as I could tell. And I worked hard. Really hard. It neither fazed nor bothered me that I'd had only two official weekends off during my first year as a Special Agent. Also, since word had gotten around that I was a hard-core runner and logged long hours in the Secret Service gym, in addition to those I spent on duty, my peers also respected me as an athlete, a humbling but gratifying honor. In short, I loved what I did, and if everyone I worked with could see that, well, that was a good thing. After completing a rigorous training program, I was finally living my dream life as a federal agent.

As I approached the car, I looked back toward the house, where I thought I saw a curtain shift. Marvin and Margaret Bush, Walker and

Marshall's parents, lived a quiet, private life. Though they had waived Secret Service protection for themselves, as minors Walker and Marshall had no such option according to the law, regardless of what their parents wanted for them. This was my first rotation protecting Walker, age two, and Marshall, age five. I would be assigned one of the two grandchildren protection details monthly, protecting either Walker and Marshall or Sam and Ellie. Each assignment would last a week, and I would spend much of the time on this particular detail sitting in a car outside their home. It was, as we said in the field, "boring but low risk."

Working at this distance from my protectees was a change from my other monthly rotation, which involved protecting Walker and Marshall's cousins, Sam and Ellie, the children of Dorothy Bush and William LeBlond. Sam was seven, and Ellie was five, and like most kids, they were active and curious. Over time, I got to know them pretty well, as my duties included taking them to school, staying at the school all day, bringing them home, and interacting with them in the afternoons and evenings, sometimes right up until bedtime. Along with several other agents, I even traveled with Sam and Ellie to Portland, Maine, when they visited their father over Christmas.

Not every agent loved travel assignments; I lived for them. The opportunity to see more of the country was one reason I'd worked tenaciously for a position with the Secret Service in the first place, and even in subzero temperatures, the trip to Maine confirmed that the effort I'd put in to completing piles of paperwork, submitting to background checks, and learning the ropes at the Federal Law Enforcement Training Center in Glynco, Georgia, had all been worth it. In Maine, I had landed a coveted day shift, which meant more activity—a plus for a rookie like me—as well as nights off to explore the town, browse the aisles of L.L.Bean's flagship store, and dip juicy hunks of local lobster into butter at any number of nice restaurants. Plus, I was partnered with the senior agent on the detail, Roy McCorkle, a truly stand-up guy who shared generously from his years of experience and taught me on-the-job skills I was just beginning to hone.

When I reached my supervisor's car, I lowered myself into the front seat—the vinyl still warm from the heater—and picked up the phone. "Hello, Mr. Basham. This is Mary Beth Wilkas."

"Hi, Mary Beth." Ralph Basham's ever-steady voice came over the line. "How's everything going in Virginia?"

Although a sense of dread lay heavy in my stomach, I spoke evenly and calmly as we made small talk for a few minutes. Then a lull in the conversation signaled that we couldn't put off discussing the reason for his call any longer.

"Look, Mary Beth," he started, "I got a call from Internal Affairs. The Service received a communication from the FBI about your application, and apparently there are some issues."

"Oh, OK, sir," I said. It was the most I could manage in the moment, as all the oxygen in the car seemed to have been sucked out. My eyes darted to the rearview mirror; my supervisor and colleagues were still huddled on the sidewalk talking. I felt a pang of envy. This was—so far, at least—a totally unexceptional day for them.

SAIC Basham took on a reassuring tone. He was, as always, calm and encouraging. "This isn't urgent, Mary Beth. Finish up in Virginia, enjoy your weekend, and come see me first thing Monday morning. Let's make it 9:00 a.m."

Enjoy your weekend? I appreciated the kindness in his suggestion, but that would be hard, if not impossible, to do. My mind was already chewing on his words: *Internal affairs? Issues? What kind of issues? Minor issues? Would the SAIC really be calling me with minor issues? Hell, no.*

When we hung up, I sat in my supervisor's car for a minute, watching a cloud of condensation form on the window with each exhale. I took a deep breath, opened the door, and walked back to my colleagues. My brief absence hadn't gone unnoticed, and the other agents, who had teased me for being one of Basham's favorites, ribbed me: Why had the boss called? What did he want? I laughed and made up a story on the spot about a misunderstanding in my file, something about my time living in Spain. My answer seemed to satisfy them, and they all got back to work.

I waited for Monday.

CHAPTER

1

When the taxi from O'Hare pulled up at my parents' house, the jet lag was just beginning to set in. After three years of living in Spain, I had boarded a plane to return to the comforts of the familiar, though my future seemed anything but certain. I wanted more than anything to start the career in federal law enforcement I had long envisioned for myself, but that prospect seemed distant and daunting. It could take months, if not years, I knew, to complete the application process and be offered a job—that is, if I even passed the battery of physical tests, the polygraph, and background checks along the way. In the meantime, I would have to wait . . . and wait.

It was a Friday evening, and the driveway of our ivy-covered Park Ridge home was empty. My parents were out having dinner with friends, but my feelings weren't hurt. After all, I hadn't told them I was coming home. As I found the house key in the same spot where it had been hidden since my six siblings and I were kids, I thought of how surprised my mom and dad would be to find me sitting on the couch, and it made me smile. I unlocked the front door and took my bags to my old bedroom, then settled myself in front of the TV to wait, exhausted but too excited to sleep.

Several hours later, when I heard their car pull up, I turned down the TV and tiptoed to the front door. When it opened, I stepped out from behind the doorway and said, "Hola!" My mother almost had a heart attack. Dad laughed and said, "MB, how are you?" We hugged, my mother gradually started to breathe again, and I told them I was home to stay. "FAN-tastic!" my dad said, and my mom, no longer quite so pale, exclaimed, "Oh, honey, that's great!" As nebulous as my future was in that moment, I knew one thing for sure: my parents would always welcome me home.

Mary Beth (row two, seat two) in first grade at Mary, Seat of Wisdom Catholic School

I'm the fifth of seven kids in my family. My brother came first, followed immediately by four girls, with only a year separating the five of us. A few years after me, my sister Nancy came along. Then, five years after that, Christine completed the family. In total, us Wilkas kids spanned a twelve-year range. Being the fifth child in a big family made me pretty independent from an early age. I learned young how to take care of myself, and I was constantly observing the people I lived with, sometimes from a *very* close vantage point. Whereas my parents and brother had their own bathrooms, my five sisters and I shared a single bathroom. Hard to imagine, I know, but we made it work—though it's not like we had a choice. For good reason, we called my mother "the General." She imposed a rigorous—and necessary—sense of order on our household, starting with hospital corners for the beds we made every morning and a white glove test of the cleaning we did on the weekends. My mom, Lois Wilkas, was a trained nurse, and although she slowed down working full-time when she started having kids, she stayed involved both as a volunteer with a number of local organizations and part-time, most notably working three days a week at a nearby home for unwed mothers and troubled girls. Our friends adored her, and I'd regularly find them sitting around our kitchen table with her as she smoked, sharing war stories from her career and lending them no-nonsense advice and a nonjudgmental ear. "Your mom is so cool," they'd tell us. *Oh, but if she were* your *mom . . .* I always thought to myself as I rolled my eyes. Sometimes I even said it out loud.

My dad, Larry Wilkas, meanwhile, took the bus to the train every morning, then took the train downtown to the Merchandise Mart, where he worked as an executive vice president in personnel—what's now called human resources—for Canteen Corporation, a foodservice company. He worked hard, and when he wasn't traveling, he was usu-ally home by five thirty, with dinner on the table by six. He was definitely a man of routine. Dad was gentle-natured and tended to defer to my mother when we brought big questions to them. I rarely saw him get bent out of shape or raise his voice, even in moments the majority of parents find stressful. While teaching me and my siblings to drive, the most he might say was, "Honey, you're about to crash, so you might want to put on the brakes."

My parents, Catholics who became more devout as they grew older, complemented each other well. Whereas my mother showed her caring by making sure we were all fed, clothed, and clean and by getting us where we needed to be each day, my dad showed his by quietly trusting me and my siblings to be our own people and to make good choices. Once when I was home from college, I told my dad I was headed downtown to meet some friends and go to a tapas bar. A year or so later, this same evening came up in conversation, and my dad admitted, "I thought you said you were going to a *topless* bar." I was baffled and embarrassed: "And you didn't say anything?" He shrugged and said, "Well, honey, it's your life." I just stared at him for a couple of seconds. That was my dad.

The rhythms of our family life were comfortingly reliable: my siblings and I moved between school, sports practice (all the Wilkas kids were athletes), and home again. My parents enrolled us in the Catholic school a block from our house from first through eighth grades, so we walked to school and sometimes came home for lunch, depending on whether my mom was working and whether my older sisters had reached an age my mom could trust them to be in charge of us. From ninth grade on, we went to the public high school a few miles away. My parents had moved to Park Ridge, a suburb about fifteen miles northwest of downtown Chicago, for the schools; education was paramount to them, and they sacrificed a lot to make sure we were well prepared for college.

Mary Beth in college at Indiana University

One way they did this was by making a deal with each of us that we couldn't refuse: we could go to any college we could get accepted to, so long as we understood that they would pay for the first two years and we would pay for the second two years. To that end, we all started working as early as we could, and at least half of each paycheck had to go to our college funds. House rules. My dad sweetened this savings plan by supplementing our contributions—if I had, say, eighty-seven bucks, he'd make it an even hundred-dollar deposit. I got my first job at thirteen, at Brown's Chicken, a Chicago-based competitor of KFC. I loved working right off the bat, so much so that when I applied to Walgreen's at age fifteen, I told them I was sixteen, their minimum age for employment. It was close to home, and I loved watching my college fund grow.

Though I didn't always have as much cash as my friends did for trips to the mall during my college years, learning financial responsibility paid dividends by the time I was out of college. I was the only one of my siblings who opted for a public school, Indiana University, and the only one who graduated debt free. My parents discouraged us from having jobs while at college, wanting us to focus instead on our studies, but summers and holidays were fair game. I socked away money as quickly as I could earn it. It was almost a personal challenge to see how much I could add to my account in any given time period. As my mother used to observe, "You can't get to the bank fast enough."

Not long after I nearly shocked my mother to death at the front door, my parents dropped their own bomb: my father had accepted a job transfer to South Carolina, they were selling our childhood home I'd just returned to, and they were moving. Soon. Another house rule was that any Wilkas kid that came back to live at home after college was expected to pay rent, which I was prepared to do, but I had hoped to have their home as a landing strip of sorts while I got my feet underneath me and some solid job prospects in my pocket. Plus, my parents were lifelong Chicagoans. The idea of them leaving everything we'd built there as a family surprised me. Though I outwardly tried to keep my cool, internally I was a bit adrift.

My parents, I'm sure, sensed my angst, because about a week later they sat me down and said, "Mary Beth, we want to give you an early birthday gift." They went on to tell me that the house sale wouldn't close for several months so I could stay there, rent free, until the new owners moved in. Holy shit. What a relief!

The Wilkas family: Tom, Judy, Mary Beth, Nancy, Larry, Lois, Christine, Anne, Peggy, 1992

I took about a week to readjust to being back in the USA and reconnect with friends, and then I got right down to business. I contacted the Chicago Field Offices of the United States Secret Service (USSS) and the Drug Enforcement Agency (DEA). Back in 1990, of course, there was no such thing as email or an online application portal. Contacting a federal agency to discuss employment took a phone call, during which I conveyed my interest in becoming a Special Agent and asked about the application process. I went downtown to the USSS and DEA offices and picked up a hard copy of Standard Form 171 (SF 171), the Application for Federal Employment. The form was short—four pages—but a little intimidating. No doubt, it would have been more intimidating had I not already completed an application to the FBI the previous year, while I was living in Spain.

I'd fallen in love with Seville in college, when I'd studied abroad there for a semester as a junior. From Spain I'd traveled all over Europe—to Portugal, France, Germany, Belgium, the Netherlands, Switzerland, Austria, Hungary, Italy, and the UK. I even popped across the Mediterranean to Tangier, Fez, and Marrakesh. Knowing there was a whole continent to explore—people to get to know, cities and towns to discover, wine and food to experience—was so exciting that I returned to my beloved Seville after graduating from IU. My plan was to spend the summer there, teaching English and improving my fluency in Spanish. That was, of course, after a month of travel in Scandinavia, a graduation gift I gave myself, after which I'd made my way back to Spain through amazing cities like Munich.

People laughed at me when I told them I planned to live in the coveted Barrio Santa Cruz, the old Jewish Quarter where the brick-paved streets were very narrow and quaint, and the patios overflowed with lush, colorful flowers. Streets I could run through or just stroll down, admiring the architecture and beauty. Everyone knew, I was told, that apartments there were pricey and almost never came up for rent, and on the off chance one did, no landlord in their right mind would rent it short-term. Rather than deter me, others' skepticism only made me more determined, and—naysayers be damned—within a week I'd landed a three-bedroom place on Calle Cespedes, where I stayed for the next three years with an array of international roommates.

Life in Spain was even more amazing than I could have imagined, and after my first big push to find employment, it seemed to find me. My work teaching English led to an internship at the US Consulate, and from there I took a job at a new language academy called the George Washington Center. Meanwhile, my own Spanish improved immensely, in part thanks to law classes I took at the nearby Universidad de Sevilla. When I got itchy at the language academy, after a year or so, I left and hung up my own shingle, so to speak. I touted myself as a freelance translator and interpreter and landed some fantastic jobs—some for just one or two days and others for one or two months. I did a short but well-paying stint with an English beer company doing marketing research with a group of young Spanish guys. All I had to do was interpret, from a separate room where they could not see me, what the participants were saying about the various beers, their preferences, and their opinion of the English beer. It was the first of many times I'd be rewarded for my initiative and confidence as a professional for hire. I wasn't afraid of striking out on my own, even as a young woman in a foreign country, because I trusted that others would recognize my competence and my commitment to doing a job right, whether we shared a native language or not. Besides, what did a mother tongue matter when I spoke Spanish almost as fluently as a native?

It was this skill—language—that I hoped would allow me to take the express route into the FBI, which normally required a minimum of three years of experience out of college to be considered for hire. However, I knew that through their language specialist program I might have a shot at bypassing what would otherwise feel like a monumental wait. Applicants with exceptional listening, reading, and spoken foreign language skills could potentially take the back door into the Bureau and become Special Agents on the early side. A year and a half out of IU, in September 1988, I felt pretty confident that I could measure up and decided to get the ball rolling.

I called the FBI's Chicago Field Office and was routed to the voice mailbox of Agent Tommy Black. My message to him probably sounded a bit odd. I explained that I was living in Spain and asked that, instead of calling me back, he please call my father in Chicago. Reliably receiving a call at my otherwise wonderful Calle Cespedes apartment could be complicated. For one thing, we had no answering machine, so I'd have to be home to catch the call. And if I wasn't home but one of my roommates was, there was no telling what might be lost in translation, as neither of them spoke English. What's more, making an international call was, in those days, a luxury I couldn't comfortably afford, so playing phone tag would be less than ideal.

Despite my strange request, within a day or two Agent Black reached out to my father, who insisted on going in person to the Chicago Field Office to retrieve the FD-646, better known as the Preliminary Application for a Special Agent Position. I completed and returned it almost as soon as it arrived in the mail, and by the end of October, I was officially a candidate in their Special Agent language specialist program.

When I came home to visit my family over Christmas that December, the FBI graciously accommodated my schedule, and I was able to take the Spanish written and oral exams two days later. In early January 1989, I received an official letter informing me I had passed both exams. My next step would be an interview with the Chicago Field Office—within the week. *Fast track indeed,* I thought. *They must be pretty desperate for Spanish-speaking agents.*

I should mention here that I learned interviewing skills from the best: my dad. From a pretty early age, I understood how to dress the part for the position I wanted, carry myself confidently, and speak intelligently to questions that might trip some people up—like where I saw myself in five years and what kind of compensation I expected. Some of this probably happened through osmosis, just observing my father conduct himself, day in and day out, like a true professional. Much of my knowledge, however, was a product of Dad's deep belief that his children (yes, all seven of them) should be self-sufficient and that with the right approach we could get almost any job. It was never too early to start preparing to join the workforce. And Larry Wilkas didn't stop at bringing this gospel to his own kids. Nope, my dad held annual seminars in our basement for us, our friends, and our cousins, complete with handouts and horror stories. We'd squeeze in between the pinball machine and the ping-pong table and learn the ins and outs of resume writing from a man who reviewed them for a living. "Don't think just because you got the interview, you've got the job," he'd always say.

Besides my dad, I had another secret weapon in my quest to become an FBI agent: Marlin Johnson, my father's coworker and the former head of the FBI's Chicago Field Office. What a fortunate coincidence, right? Starting in high school, when I'd first become interested in joining federal law enforcement, Mr. Johnson and I would meet at least once a year. I'd make the hour-long trek downtown, and Dad would walk me through the entire floor of their company offices to Mr. Johnson's office, introducing me to his colleagues as we went: "This is my daughter that wants to be the Charlie's Angel!" (As the father of six daughters, he had to set me apart somehow, right?) I'd sit across from Marlin Johnson at his big desk and ask question after question. Any question I had, he would either answer or call up one of his buddies in the Chicago Field Office. He'd put the phone on speaker and say, "Hey, this is Marlin. I have a young lady in front of me who's gonna make a great agent one day, and she has a question and I don't know the answer." Talking with Mr. Johnson gave me a lot of confidence and made the job seem possible, attainable, and real.

Armed with an insider's perspective and my dad's contagious determination, I arrived at my FBI interview feeling good, looking the part, and ready to enter a field I'd dreamed about working in since my junior year of high school. My dad wasn't wrong—I *did* want to be a Charlie's Angel, and since that wasn't possible, becoming an FBI agent would be the next best thing.

Now, I'm not immune to nerves, but all things considered, during my interview I kept a level head, trusted my preparation, and answered my interviewer's questions as honestly as I could. Much of our discussion focused on my answers from the FD-140, the FBI Application for Employment, which I was only given after my FD-646 (the preliminary application) had been approved. The interviewer requested clarification on a few issues, and I took my time in responding, making sure my answers were complete and accurate. Specifically, he had a few questions about my college years, my time in Spain, and where I had traveled in Europe. I wouldn't say I have perfect recall, but it's definitely well above average; I felt confident that whatever details I offered about my past would square with what the FBI would find, if they chose to look into it more. As I walked out of the Chicago Field Office, my father's words of wisdom—"Don't think just because you got the interview, you've got the job"—floated through my mind, but it was a fleeting thought. I knew I'd kicked ass.

A few days later, Agent Tommy Black, the person I'd initially been in touch with at the agency, called me at my parents' house. Still riding a high from the interview earlier that week—I was that much closer to watching the puzzle pieces of my life come together—I gave my mom a hopeful thumbs-up as she handed me the phone. She and my father, I knew, were both excited to see me land something I'd worked so long and so hard for.

Agent Black started by thanking me for coming in and for my candor and honesty, both on my application and during my interview. As soon as the words left his mouth, my Spider sense started to tingle. Had I been *too* candid? Unfortunately, he said, the FBI had decided to eliminate me as a candidate for Special Agent. To understand why, you should know that the FBI has deal breakers, no matter how great a candidate is otherwise. There are nine reasons someone can be automatically disqualified from employment with the Bureau. These range from failing to pay income taxes or child support, to having a felony conviction, to participating in activities designed to overthrow the US government by force.

And then there's the drug policy.

Now, if the FBI eliminated every potential agent who'd ever smoked a little marijuana, they would have to pass over an awful lot of otherwise excellently qualified candidates. Because the Bureau knew this, they allowed a certain number of "experimental" uses of marijuana. What that magic number was, however, no one applying to the FBI knew.

In the official FBI application (FD-140), under Personal Declarations, question three asked, "Do you use or have you ever used such items as marijuana, hashish, cocaine, LSD, amphetamines, heroin, or drugs of a similar nature?" I answered "yes," and then, as instructed, I described the details:

a.   Drug – marijuana, hashish

b.   How taken – smoked

c.   Circumstances – experimenting with friends

d.   How many times used – 4

e.   First time used – 5/82

f.   Last time used – 5/87

During my interview, I'd been prodded a bit further on the circumstances around my hash use. I explained that I had only experimented with it while living in Spain because it was decriminalized there and was used, I thought, as casually as marijuana among Spaniards. Due, in part, to high unemployment, crime, and heroin use, Spain's government had, in the early 1980s, decided to distinguish between hard and soft drugs and to enforce the former more energetically than the latter. Law enforcement in the US also distinguished between hard and soft drugs but took a different stance, I was learning, when it came to hashish. Although, like marijuana, hash is part of the cannabis family, it typically contains a higher level of THC, or tetrahydrocannabinol, than marijuana. THC is the psychoactive constituent of cannabis. Because hash can contain up to four times the amount of THC as marijuana, it's considered a harder drug in the United States. And that, my friends, was my personal deal breaker. No hard drug use, even if experimental, was allowed at that time if you wanted to become a federal agent in the FBI. So much for acing my interview.

I was crushed, but I'm not the kind of person who wallows. I also don't easily let go of something I really want. In this case, I wasn't going to accept no for an answer—not without a fight, anyway. When I hung up with Agent Black, I had a week left in Chicago before my return to Spain, a week I now planned to spend at the public library in Park Ridge, drafting my appeal to the FBI. I spent three straight days researching everything there was to know about marijuana in the United States. I also researched Spanish law as it pertained to the sale, possession, and use of hashish. Then I spent another three days writing and rewriting my appeal. My argument revolved around three main points:

- According to recent research, the marijuana coming into and being sold and used in the United States was equally as, if not more, potent in THC levels than hashish.

- Despite the fact that hashish typically contains a higher level of THC, I, like most people, smoked a very small amount mixed with tobacco. Therefore, the psychoactive drug content, THC, would likely have been equivalent to or even less than that in a typical marijuana joint.

- Finally—and this, I felt, was central to my argument— hashish had been decriminalized in Spain since 1982. Possessing and using hash in private areas was legal.

I reread my letter of appeal about fifty times, made a few copies, and sent it off. Two weeks later, my father called me in Spain to say he'd received a letter from my designated FBI personnel officer. The letter acknowledged my appeal but upheld the Bureau's original decision to disqualify me as a candidate due to my "self-admitted usage of a controlled substance." The final line of the letter stated, "I know that this decision will be disappointing to you, but trust that you will understand the FBI's decision in this matter."

Disappointed? I was beyond disappointed. I was devastated. I mean, hell, I wholeheartedly thought I was going to be an FBI agent, whether it was through the language specialist program or through other channels.

I thought back to meeting with Marlin Johnson at my dad's office. Looking back, I didn't even know him that well, but for some reason then—and now—I really had this feeling that I wanted to make him proud. And my dad, too. I was young, a teenager, and I'd told them I wanted to be an FBI agent, and they'd assured me that yes, of course I would be. They made it seem attainable, like it was going to happen, like it was going to be who I was.

"Mary Beth," they said, "you're going to be a great agent. They're going to be lucky to have you."

And I thought, *What could stop me?*

Well, apparently a personnel officer at the FBI and a youthful indiscretion. A difference in international drug laws and a little bit of hash. That was what stopped me. And now I wasn't going to be an FBI agent. It was a blow, but I could deal with it. But what the heck was I going to be? My mother, my father, Marlin Johnson, the personnel officer— none of them could answer that for me.

So I laced up my shoes, and I set out on a run, ready to figure out my way forward. From my home in the Jewish Quarter, I headed down Calle Santa Maria la Blanca to the amazing Murillo Gardens, which took only a matter of minutes. Then, with the sun blazing down, I ran toward the Parque de María Luisa, where there were some water fountains. The only time I had to run in Sevilla was during siesta, which was also the hottest time of day.

All along my route, the Seville oranges were in bloom. When ripened, the flesh of the oranges was far too bitter to eat, and the fruit, which looked so lovely, would lie unwanted on the ground, littering the *calles* and *avenidas* of the city. Now, though, the trees were blossoming, and an incredible aroma hung over the streets.

I passed the university on my right and the monument to El Cid Campeador—the valiant. I then made my way through the park, past the fountains, and around the various plazas. I ran down by the river for a bit, but it was crowded with tourists. Finally, I headed back home, exhausted but with my head now clear.

Still smarting and now sweating, I told myself that the FBI was just not meant to be. I needed to move on. No wallowing, remember.

Over the years, when people have asked me how I became a Secret Service agent, I've told them, "I applied." By that, I mean I filled out the mounds of paperwork. That's not all I did, of course, but forms—so many forms—are a huge part of getting the job. In May 1990, I sat down at my parents' kitchen table in Chicago and got to work on SF 171, the mother of all forms. And just in case you're thinking, *What's the big deal? It's a four-page application,* there are a lot of people who don't even make it into the candidate consideration process because completing this first form is such a huge pain in the ass. You can't schmooze your way into a role with the federal government; you have to follow procedure.

Pen in hand, I started to list everywhere I'd worked in the past ten years, what I'd studied in college, my special skills and accomplishments, three references who were neither relatives nor former supervisors—and on and on it went. Via certified mail, I shipped one copy to the DEA and one copy to the Secret Service, both on May 23. Within a few weeks, I'd heard back from the Secret Service with instructions to set up an interview with the Chicago Field Office. This was, essentially, the first hurdle in the USSS process and determined whether I would even be invited to begin my walk on the bed of hot coals—also known as the long and challenging hiring process.

In July, I met with Bill Tebbe, SAIC of the Chicago Field Office. He was very welcoming and relaxed throughout the interview, which eased some of my tension and allowed me to be more, well, me. He complimented me on having lived in a foreign country and having learned the language and culture, saying that was very appealing to the Service. At the same time, he let me know that, since I had lived, worked, and traveled extensively overseas, my background check would take longer than most and that I should expect to wait quite a while for my application to be processed—up to two years.

Two years? At twenty-five—hell, at any age—that's a long time. By this point, my parents had said farewell to the Park Ridge house where I was still living, thanks to their generosity, and the rooms were pretty empty. Some six weeks back from Spain, I felt like I was neither here nor there. I had good prospects but no job; I had grown up in Chicago, but most of my friends from high school had scattered; I needed an income badly. More than that, I needed a focus, a sense of purpose, and I wanted that in the form of a job. For the first time in my life, I was a little lonely. But again, I don't lollygag; I act. If I was going to wait two years to hear back from the Secret Service, I was going to spend that time doing something worthwhile.

The daughter of one of my mother's bridge friends invited me to Washington, DC, where she worked for the US Agency for International Development (USAID). No problem, she could set up some interviews for me, she said. By August, I'd landed a job as a program assistant with the Center for Democracy. Before I made the move to DC, I contacted the Chicago Field Office of the Secret Service and was told that my application would be transferred to the Washington Field Office, and—surprise, surprise—this transfer would likely slow things down. Oh well. At least I wouldn't be cooling my heels.

Bill Tebbe called to tell me he thought I should take the Treasury Enforcement Agent (TEA) Exam, which was the next step in the application process, before leaving Chicago. I rushed out, bought an exam guide, and crammed like crazy. The TEA exam is a long, dense, difficult test used to evaluate candidates for not only the Secret Service but also the ATF, the Customs Service, the Border Patrol, and the IRS. Tebbe made special arrangements for me to take it on an expedited schedule by myself in the Chicago Field Office, and fortunately I passed. "You know, not a high percentage of people pass the TEA exam the first time around," he told me. "Jeez, I'm glad you didn't tell me that *before* I took the exam," I replied. We both laughed.

In DC, I moved into a beautiful place in the Cleveland Park neighborhood with two roommates. My job at the Center for Democracy allowed me to speak Spanish almost every day, and given my travel history and language skills, I quickly got pegged as the in-house Latin American expert, alongside Pam, who was my boss. It was a big role for someone who was new to the organization, considering that our primary mission was to assist in carrying out election monitoring all over the world. I was focused on all facets of organizing, confirming, and educating my election monitoring delegations, and that meant being tenacious about getting election observers from all over the world to commit to the missions.

Election monitoring in a foreign country is a fascinating process. First and foremost, organizations such as ours must receive an invitation from the country holding the elections. An election observation mission entails physical monitoring of the candidates and the electoral process over a period of time, as well as observation of election-day proceedings. National and international observers who are invited and choose to participate have the responsibility to record and report their observations, ask pertinent and necessary questions throughout the process, and—this one is especially important—not intervene in the process or directly prevent election fraud. The goal of any election observation mission is to declare the elections "free and fair."

The job took me to Guatemala and El Salvador many times, and I loved it. On a trip to monitor the legislative elections in El Salvador in 1991, I had a fascinating encounter that went beyond the usual. As I sat at the hotel bar with Pam drinking coffee and discussing strategy, I noticed a guy at the other end of the bar trying to get my attention. We tried to ignore him, but he kept gesturing. Was he drunk? A few minutes later, Pam and I left and went around the corner to the lobby to meet our boss and some colleagues for a meeting. As we sat on a couch mapping out our plans for the days ahead, particularly what we were going to talk about with one of the presidential candidates later that day, I felt a hot puff of breath on my neck.

"Does the DEA mean anything to you?" someone whispered into my ear.

The guy from the bar! It clicked immediately. Holy shit! Several months earlier, I'd met him during my panel interview with the DEA. They'd called me in to grill me—I mean talk to me—around the same time the Secret Service had. This man had come into the conference room unexpectedly in the middle of my interview, casually sat down, and launched into a rapid-fire conversation with me in Spanish. Fifteen minutes into our back-and-forth, he stood and said, "I could work with this woman," and walked out. I'd been tested, and I'd passed. And there he was, standing behind the couch I was sitting on in a hotel in San Salvador. I mean, come on!

I excused myself from the team meeting and went to speak with him. He was extremely kind and said he could tell I hadn't recognized him. He asked me how my application process was going with the DEA and explained that he was in El Salvador on an undercover assignment. He went on to tell me that he had to make sure I knew who he was because, if I had an "aha moment" about his identity and called him out in the crowded hotel bar as a DEA agent, it would have potentially put both of us in serious danger. It dawned on me what a lucky thing it was that I hadn't recognized him at first. At that moment I realized what my life would be like as a Special Agent—full of danger and intrigue, which was exactly what I was looking for.

As it turns out, it was looking for me, too. On January 14, 1991, not even eight months after sending in my initial application, I received a call from a Special Agent in the Washington Field Office (WFO) of the Secret Service to set up the panel interview. The man who called me, Lou Soucy, was so kind it caught me off guard. We spent quite a bit of time talking, like old friends catching up on our lives. Lou told me he had spoken with the SAIC in the Chicago Field Office and said that the SAIC there had been impressed with me—so much so that he had personally asked Lou to take good care of me because I was a "top-notch candidate." Lou told me a little about the hiring process, and we set up a panel interview for January 23. He asked that I complete and bring—you guessed it—more forms, this time unsigned copies of the SF 86, Questionnaire for Sensitive Positions; the SF 86A, Supplemental Investigative Data; and, last but not least, TD F 67-32.5, the Authorization for Release of Information. I would then sign them on the day of my panel interview in front of him, a witness. These questionnaires went even deeper into my previous employment and travel, places I had lived, my financial history, my drug and alcohol use, and every single one of my family members. They also asked questions like whether I had a personal or continuing contact with a citizen of a Soviet, Soviet bloc, or communist country. (The USSR had just collapsed a month prior, and the Cold War was still in its death throes.)

With my paperwork in order, I polished up my interviewing skills and prepared for another shot at federal employment. Though the Center for Democracy had been a terrific experience, the life of danger and intrigue I'd always wanted finally felt within reach.

"So, Mary Beth . . ." Sitting across a large table from me with two other agents, also panel members, Lou Soucy shuffled his notes. "Let me get this straight. You went to Spain after you graduated college, at the age of 21, found a place to live, found a variety of good jobs, and lived there, on your own, without any help from your parents, for three years?"

Is this a trick question? I held my breath, unsure what he was getting at.

"Yes, sir," I said.

"You know," he said, clearing his throat a bit, "I spent two years in the Paris office for the Secret Service, and they did everything for me—moved me, gave me the job, set up a place to live for my wife and me—and I still struggled. I am beyond impressed by your initiative."

Whew. "Thank you, sir," I said with a nod and a humble smile.

The next day, when Lou called to tell me I'd advanced to the polygraph, I literally started jumping up and down. I was that much closer.

A few weeks later, I found myself sitting in a small room with electrodes attached to me as a man named Jack, who had reviewed the questions and my responses on the SF 86 and SF 86A, asked me question after question about my past. Afterward, he delivered me to Lou's office. Lou, brows furrowed, asked, "How'd she do?" Jack took a full beat before smiling and saying, "She's good to go." I inwardly sighed with relief. "You're almost there, kid," Lou said encouragingly. I just had a medical exam, a drug screening, and background check to go. The first item, I passed no problem. For the drug screening, I had to urinate into a cup while a woman observed me. Awkward, but I wasn't shy. Again, I passed, no problem. Just one more major hurdle— the background investigation. Once that launched, my parents and I began hearing from people, including former neighbors, that federal agents had come around asking about me.

I was in Miami for the night, on my way back from El Salvador, when I got a message from my office that the Washington Field Office of the Secret Service had called and for me to call them back. Could this be the good news? No way, it was way too soon for that. More likely, some issue had cropped up with my background check that required clarification. *Don't get your hopes up, Mary Beth. Remember: two years.*

From my hotel window I could see the pool and, beyond it, Biscayne Bay. The turquoise water shimmered as boats of all sizes cruised by. *This life is a very good life*, I told myself, steeling myself against disappointment. *Everything happens for a reason.* I sat down on the bed, picked up the phone, and dialed the Washington Field Office. I'd barely heard the ringtone when the Special Agent who'd called me answered.

"Hi, Mary Beth. How are you doing today?" he said brightly.

Unprepared for his chatty tone, I answered, a bit warily, "Um, good. How are you?"

He chuckled. "I'm calling to offer you a job as a Special Agent with the United States Secret Service."

I almost dropped the phone.

I'd been so prepared for a long wait, no news, or bumps along the way—I'd been prepared to wait for *two years*—and here I was, ten months into the application process, getting the call. I couldn't believe it. It was really happening. I'd just landed my dream job. Holy shit!

CHAPTER
2

WASHINGTON, DC

1991

I was watching an exit that might only ever be used by the president as a backup to a backup. It was important—life-or-death—work, and it was also just me, an elevator door, a long hallway, and flickering fluorescent lights. I'd been standing there for a couple of hours.

It was my job to do whatever I could to be ready, but still, my mind wandered. I considered talking to myself, just to break the monotony. My gaze scanned back and forth down the long hallway. I looked to the elevator door. The long hallway. The flickering fluorescent tube. The elevator. I was aware. But was I 100 percent alert? I think so. At least, I tried to be.

This was the job. The tedium it entailed was starting to sink in. That didn't make me like it any less, but it was a fact to be reckoned with. How was I going to deal with the boredom of a post like this and still keep on my toes? I knew I couldn't let my guard down. I couldn't start talking to myself. Not out loud anyway.

As a new agent, for the first year or so, you get the crappy, boring posts and are pulled first off your other duties for every protection assignment. It's low-man-on-the-totem-pole stuff, like working check forgery, which is incredibly boring and tedious. Essentially, you're undergoing on-the-job training, an experience every new agent goes through. It's a rite of passage.

For this assignment, I was part of the second ring of what's called the concentric rings of security. The agents in the first ring—the presidential protection detail—were responsible for guarding the president 24/7 when he was on the move. It's all they did. As a field office agent, I was supplementing them. There were also fellow field office agents, local police, the counterassault team, counter-snipers on top of nearby buildings, an ambulance, and one or two advance agents at a local hospital, all just in case anything—God forbid—happened.

If someone breached an outer layer of security, I might not know: those agents and officers could be dead. If anyone got to me, in the second layer of security, something had gone seriously wrong. If they got past me, shit would hit the fan. The president of the United States would be under attack. And that, right there, was my motivation.

Suffice to say, I would not let anyone get into that elevator or even near it for that matter. I would stay alert. How to stand for long periods of time and remain alert is a crucial skill for new agents in the USSS to learn. What they'd drilled into us during our nearly twenty weeks of training here in Washington, DC, and Beltsville, Maryland, made sense now that I was on the job: the enemy has to be lucky once; targets, every time. It would be one of the many lessons that I assimilated as a rookie.

Washington, DC, 1991, US Secret Service Agent training graduation

As I stood by that elevator door, I heard a bing. The doors opened, and George H. W. Bush, the president of the United States, walked out. One of his agents made eye contact with me and gave me a half-smile of acknowledgment. The presidential protection detail had decided to use an alternative exit—my exit—after all. No one had told me, but of course they didn't need to; the Presidential Protection Detail uses a different radio channel than us field office agents. My job was to watch the elevator and make sure nobody got on from my floor.

Later, the mission complete without incident, the president safe and sound, a feeling came over me more powerful than any boredom. I knew I had done something that mattered that day.

The United States Secret Service is one of the oldest federal law enforcement agencies in the country. It was founded in 1865 as a branch of the US Department of the Treasury and was originally created to combat the counterfeiting of US currency, which was a serious problem at the time. In fact, following the Civil War, it was estimated that one-third to one-half of the currency in circulation was counterfeit. Then, in 1901, following the assassination of President William McKinley in Buffalo, New York, the Secret Service was tasked with its second mission: the protection of the president. Eventually, in early 2003, when federal law enforcement was reorganized after 9/11, the Secret Service was moved out of the Department of the Treasury to become part of the newly established Department of Homeland Security.

Thus the Secret Service is tasked with a dual mission: investigations and protection. Investigative responsibilities fall under the general category of financial crimes and cover counterfeit US currency and other US Treasury securities; forgery or theft of US Treasury checks, bonds, or other securities; credit card fraud; identity fraud; and certain other crimes affecting federally insured financial institutions. Like any law enforcement job, there's a lot of pressure for agents to be involved in and stay on top of the investigative mission of the USSS.

But the stakes are even higher when you consider the protection mission. The Secret Service has primary jurisdiction to investigate threats against any and all Secret Service protectees. That means ensuring the safety of the nation's most important leaders, past and present, and their families: the president, vice president, and their families, as well as former presidents. They are also responsible for protecting visiting heads of state on official business. Additionally, the Secret Service is authorized by law to protect major presidential and vice-presidential candidates who become the respective primary winners, and their spouses, within 120 days of a general presidential election.

The protection mission of the Secret Service not only brings a high-stress element to the job, it also demands a significant amount of time away from home. The fact is, being a Secret Service agent, whether you are male or female, is much more than a job. It can become all-encompassing, especially if you want to move up in the agency. That takes total dedication, a lot of hours on the job, and very little time for a personal life. Agents are on call constantly, and the world is unpredictable. Say the president is in the hospital. Or maybe there's some crisis that happens overseas and the president needs to rush off to meet an ambassador or prime minister. Or an emergency meeting of the Cabinet is called. It could be 2:00 p.m. or 2:00 a.m. The USSS needs to make sure enough agents are ready and able to report for duty and to ensure the president's safety, no matter what. It's us field office agents who are called to supplement the Presidential Protection Detail in any and all such circumstances.

Here's what it boils down to: choice. No one forces you to become an agent, and no one forces you to stay. You just have to know that, if you choose to stay, you will make plenty of sacrifices. Those of us who do choose it know the cost, are often reminded, and we also know how important the work is. And that makes us feel the need, the desire, and the determination to do it that much more.

In 1991, there weren't a lot of women who were able or willing to do that. Even today, women are the primary caregivers in a high percentage of households and are typically the ones that leave their careers to have and raise children, or at least take on the majority of parenting responsibilities. This was also true in the Secret Service—women left to start families or to get married and start careers that were less demanding, less stressful, and less prone to constant time and travel away from home.

In 1970, Phyllis Shantz was the first woman sworn into the Executive Protection Service, which became the Uniformed Division of the USSS. The next year, equal employment laws were modified, and employers were no longer allowed to discriminate on the basis of sex. So it was that shift, 106 years after the agency was established, when Shantz, along with Laurie Anderson, Sue Ann Baker, Kathryn Clark, and Holly Hufschmidt, made history and became the first female Special Agents in the USSS.

From what I know of the first group of female agents in the USSS, their experiences and mine were as different as night and day. The service didn't know what to do with women at that time. They wore skirts and carried purses and were primarily assigned to protect only the wives and daughters of diplomats. These women were definitely pathfinders, and without them and the people who helped them push forward, women still wouldn't be considered "equals," to the extent that they are.

It probably won't be a surprise that as a rookie agent in 1991, a full two decades after the "first five" were sworn in as female USSS Agents, I still had to prove myself to pretty much everyone in the field office. There were agents, even in my own training class, who still believed women did not have a place in the Service and that we had ruined "the good old boys' club." In fact, one of the most memorable comments I heard from an older male agent was, "Buicks, booze, and broads. Those were the good old days. And bringing women into the Service ruined that." I just smiled and said, "I'd say we are the best decision the Service ever made, but that's just me." At least my response got a chuckle out of the guy.

Even though I went through the same application process, had been through the same training, and was doing the same job every day, I was still treated as though I were being tested by many of the other (male) agents. It was as if the rookie male agents were automatically assumed to be worthy and belong, but the other rookie females and I still had to prove ourselves. Female agents were scrutinized extra closely, and any perceived flaws were noted and exploited. It was also understood that if female agents were better than their male counterparts at something— especially shooting, defensive tactics, or physical fitness—many of those men would be pissed. But hell, I thrive on challenge, especially when the stakes are high. And so I proved myself. Every day. And I loved it. It motivated me like nothing else, and to watch my fellow (male) agents come around to seeing and treating me as an equal was almost entertaining.

To be clear, I signed up for the organization knowing what I was getting into. If I had let what people thought of me affect me or dictate how I was going to live my life, I would have been married at twenty-one (and gotten divorced), stayed in my hometown (and become depressed), and gone into sales (and been miserable). Instead, I joined the Secret Service, and I proved myself, over and over again, though it wasn't always easy. Not that I wanted it to be easy. What would be the point of that? I often reminded myself of something my mother said: "Nothing worth having comes easy, but it's worth the effort."

For my first assignment, I considered myself fortunate to be posted in the Washington Field Office, the dynamic epicenter of USSS action. First and foremost, our primary protectees—the president and vice president—lived and worked in DC. Then, there was always a steady stream of foreign dignitaries coming into and moving through DC.

That meant, on any given day, you were coordinating with many of your fellow field office agents, presidential and vice presidential protective teams, USSS Uniformed Division officers, DC police, Capitol Police, Andrews Air Force Base personnel, foreign embassies, hotel staff, DC residents, tourists, and whoever else might be involved in any way, shape, or form in investigative or protective missions.

In addition to President Bush and Vice President Quayle and their spouses, two of President Bush's kids lived in the DC area—Marvin and Dorothy—and WFO was responsible for the protection of their families too. When foreign dignitaries (we called them "foreign digs") came to DC for official visits, they were given Secret Service protection from the time they landed in the United States to the time they left the country. As far as lodging, they either stayed at Blair House, which is the president's guesthouse across the street from the White House, or they stayed in a posh hotel. If they chose to stay in a hotel, which was a typical choice if they were traveling with a large entourage, WFO agents were assigned to set up and operate the command post in that hotel. I was on the job for less than two weeks before I was setting up a command post with another female WFO agent. At first I thought, *What the hell do I know about command posts?* But, as I quickly learned, there is nothing like on-the-job training to help you really understand and learn the nuances of your responsibilities.

Though DC was a hotbed of protection work, most new agents were assigned to the check forgery squad. We still had to do our share of protection work, but, at a very minimum, we were obligated procedurally to keep our investigative cases updated; ideally, we'd close them, but it was a delicate balance. Especially as a newbie, I didn't necessarily know what I was going to be doing on any given day or why, and to be honest, it took a while to figure out how to master the juggling act of protective and investigative work. We were expected to work sixty hours a week, which sometimes turned into eighty hours.

You'd have to check your mailbox—it was 1991, so, yes, a physical one—near the entrance to the office at least two or three times a day to find out if you'd been given any protection assignments. It was a rare day that I wasn't sent out on a protection mission in DC, at Andrews Air Force Base, or even somewhere halfway across the country, like Dallas.

One morning I arrived to an empty mailbox. Somehow, no last-minute protection assignments had been placed in there from Protective Operations the night before. Even more shocking, there was nothing, not even a short-term assignment at Andrews, waiting for me when I got in. Finally, I had some time to really dig in to one of the check forgery investigations that I'd been given. I hustled to my desk, where I pulled a file off of the growing stack. I grabbed the phone, ready to make some calls to set up interviews, and recruited a fellow agent to accompany me (those were the rules—you could not conduct investigative fieldwork alone). With any luck, I'd be able to write some status reports by the end of the day. Not exactly my idea of fun, but it would be a relief to make some progress. I started dialing.

But, alas, it was not to be, not that day anyway.

"Mary Beth? You speak Spanish, right?"

I looked up mid-dial to see one of the older agents standing by my desk. I slowly placed the handset back on the phone.

We both knew that I—and this still amazes me to this day—was the only agent in the entire DC office who spoke Spanish at the time. This agent was doing some advance work for a foreign dignitary coming in from South America, and he wanted to make sure he would be able to communicate with the embassy staff.

The older agent said to me, "Mary Beth, you know if you help me on this one, you are going to be stuck doing this with other agents in the future, so think hard about your answer." You've got to love someone who is so honest upfront. I smiled, squinted my eyes like I was really thinking about it, and, of course, I went with him.

I quickly became known as the go-to person for "everything Spanish" as they used to say. If someone needed help translating a document, they looked for me. If a call came into WFO and the person only spoke Spanish, it was passed to me. I was also asked to help out when other agents were interviewing suspects or witnesses that spoke Spanish, especially when they claimed to not speak English. The suspect would say, "No hablo Ingles," expecting that the gringo interviewing them would just give up. It was always funny to register their responses when I would say, without missing a beat, "No hay problema. Hablo Español."

As I began to get comfortable with the rhythms of life as an agent, I learned that even the most mundane operations present different challenges for men and women in the field. Consider going to the bathroom: male agents have it easier. They don't have to take any of their stuff off. As a woman, I'd have to take my gun out of my holster to use a restroom. Of course, no training covered that. Once, early on, I put my gun on the back of the toilet, did my business, washed my hands, and walked out, realizing as I was walking through the door that I had left my gun on the back of the toilet. I did a quick one-eighty, casually re-entered the stall I had just left, picked up my gun, and put it back in my holster. And then I exhaled and shook my head at myself. Nothing had come even close to happening—it had only been a few seconds—but the gravity of what *could* have happened shook me. What if I had left without my weapon? What if something happened and I needed it? Would that be the difference between my protectee's life and death? What if someone had found it? What if the wrong person had found it? Misplacing a weapon wasn't something the USSS (rightly so) had a lot of tolerance for.

As silly as it seems, you have to learn where to put your gun when you use a bathroom. There aren't a lot of options, which is why many women end up switching to shoulder holsters, but that takes a whole other set of training. We were trained with hip holsters, and if you switch, you've got to be sure that in a crisis your muscle memory will tell you to go to the new place—your shoulder, not your hip. Then there's all the other equipment you are carrying on your belt that you have to keep secured: handcuffs, loaded magazines, an extendable baton, and maybe pepper spray. It's amazing how complicated a simple trip to the bathroom can become.

The truth is, though, I found very few negatives in being female in the Secret Service; in fact, I found just the opposite—there were many upsides. There were plenty of gentlemen in the Service, and many of them treated us with respect and admiration. And maybe it doesn't seem like it's a big deal, but because there were so few women and the locker rooms were separated by gender, we had a lot more space to ourselves. That might not have been much of an advantage in the field, but we took our victories where we could get them.

Being a female agent put you in a far more elite group than being a male agent. When I became a Secret Service agent, there were approximately two thousand agents total and less than 10 percent of them, or around one hundred eighty agents, were women. I can't tell you how many times I heard people say, "Oh, I didn't know there were *female* Secret Service agents." Instead of finding that insulting, I found it hugely flattering, and I felt even more proud.

Also, most of the female Secret Service agents I met and worked with were extremely impressive in terms of their skills, professionalism, and athleticism. That was not always true for the men. Because we felt like we had to prove ourselves, the women kept themselves in shape and on their toes. Challenge is a great motivator. And female agents stuck together for the most part and supported each other.

My colleagues in DC included two women I'd gone through training with, Jeanne and Tamara, as well as other women agents: Betsy, Paula, Cindy, Linda, and Renee. Sometimes I'd see them regularly in the office, but on any given day, any of us could be out in the field. I didn't necessarily spend much time with my fellow agents on duty: I got my assignment, took my post, and that was it. Because the stakes were so high—not only were we charged with protecting these incredibly high-level people, but I was a rookie at my dream job, and a woman to boot—even a small screwup could become a desperate situation. At times like that, the support of a friendly female coworker could mean the world.

One day, I had duty on a secondary motorcade, a kind of ghost motorcade, for a foreign dig. It was another case of providing a backup so that the enemy, if there were one, wouldn't know whether the protectee was leaving through the front door or the back or somewhere in between. It wasn't quite a decoy, because, like that elevator door, it might actually get used. That kind of preparation, which allows for agile responses, is so critical.

Like a lot of rookie assignments, this one involved sitting around for long periods of time. Eventually, I needed a break. Normally, another agent would head over to where I was and give me a "push," also known as a break. In this case, I was simply given five minutes to do what I needed to do. After radioing in and finally getting the OK, I jumped out of the vehicle, knowing I had a very limited amount of time to go to the bathroom and get back to the car. The keys, I thought, were in my pants pocket, but when I got up, I experienced one of those moments where you can't believe what's happening even as it's happening. I watched as the keys dropped from my lap and fell straight through a sewer grate. All I could think was, *Are you fucking kidding me?*

There I was, a US Secret Service agent, graduate of the best training academy in the world, handed all of the resources of the US government, and entrusted with protecting major VIPs, and I couldn't hold on to the keys to my government-issued vehicle.

In retrospect, it was almost comical, but it didn't feel that way in the moment. The whole detail is on the protectee's timeline and the detail leader's protocol. What would happen if the decision was made to use this motorcade? The dignitary (and the whole team) could appear at any moment, ready to go. Even in the best-case scenario, all of WFO would find out about my screwup, and I'd go from promising rookie to office joke. I would never live it down.

It wasn't going to be easy to tell the detail leader what had happened. So I didn't. I knew it was an enormous risk, on many levels, but I decided to take it. To me, at least in that moment, there was no other option. I took a deep breath and unclipped my radio from my belt. I twisted the little knob on top and to the right from the channel the protection detail was using to the channel we used to communicate with the field office.

"Washington, this is Wilkas."

"Go ahead Wilkas, this is Washington," came the voice of Becky Ediger.

Oh. My. God. The depth of relief I felt was tremendous. Becky was the agent I was desperately hoping to get in touch with. It was after hours, and I knew she was on duty, but I wasn't sure she'd be available. I immediately exhaled. "Becky, this is Mary Beth Wilkas. I need your help."

We switched to another channel so no one else could hear our conversation. I quickly explained my situation.

"I'll be right there, Mary Beth," she responded.

I have no idea who took over for Becky back at WFO—I was in an adrenaline fog and not able to think beyond cleaning up my own mess. And although it felt like an hour, Becky was there in less than ten minutes. She just appeared, handed me a set of car keys, and said, "Don't worry about it, nobody will ever know." You better believe I was grateful—grateful she saved my ass and grateful she never said a word about it, not to other agents and not to me. That was Becky. Humble, committed, incredibly competent, and always supportive.

I was not particularly careless in those days; to the contrary, I was pretty squared away, hyperaware even. I thought that there was no room for mistakes in this job. But mistakes happen, as I learned, especially when you have worked twelve-plus hours and haven't had a day off in weeks, especially when you're a newbie. When seconds matter and lives are on the line, you have to learn to live with the consequences of your screwups. More important, you have to learn how to fix them—fast.

Along with mortifying mistakes, there were also fun, light moments—like getting starstruck. For me, it happened at least twice. And it's not over who you might think. Because I had spent nearly four years living in Spain and it held a huge place in my heart, I was thrilled to be in the command post for the official visit of the president of Spain, Felipe González. I was able to converse with the Spanish protection agents in their language, which was unusual for them, and they kindly introduced me to President González, telling him I'd lived in his hometown for four years. Epic.

The other time was when I was assigned to the motorcade for the first lady. I drove what's called the follow car for Barbara Bush's detail on a rainy day, aggressively protecting her limo. I thought the world of Barbara Bush; she was classy, confident, and down to earth, and she was devoted to inspiring causes—like her work with individuals with AIDS, which was the reason for that day's trip. As I drove, I kept alternating between excitement that someone I admired so much was right in front of me and worry that I'd embarrass myself by getting too close with my vehicle and hitting her bumper. Fortunately, I kept my cool and carried out my assignment without incident.

As I began to thrive under pressure, I found that I was learning quickly, and the work was getting more interesting—and more exciting. I was now able to focus on the real challenges of being a USSS Agent, and I started to see moments of real danger in the USSS, particularly on investigations.

"Ooh, Wilkas, I heard your friend Ron's been looking for you again."

At my desk in the Washington Field Office, I tried to roll my eyes as little as possible as one of the other agents needled me. Ron Malfi was one of the assistants to the Special Agent in Charge (ATSAIC) and the revered and enigmatic leader of the counterfeiting squad within WFO. He had been pushing the head of the field office to send me over to his team because of my ability with Spanish. The chief just kept saying, "She's too young. She's gotta get more experience." Besides, I was still assigned to the check forgery squad. But Malfi kept asking and kept pushing—it's who he was—to the point that some of the people in my squad teased me a little bit. I wasn't going to let childish antics get to me or get in the way of an opportunity I really wanted. I shook my head at the agent messing with me and turned back to the report I was typing up, another piece of the seemingly endless trail of red tape that went along with being an agent.

A lot of agents wanted to work counterfeiting, in no small part because of Malfi. He was street-smart, practical, and tough. He had a great clearance rate for investigations. He wasn't just commanding; he was an ass-kicker. He brought bad guys down himself, leading raids out in the field rather than sitting in his office and running things from behind his desk. That was unusual for the head of any squad in the Secret Service.

Of course, not everyone was looking for that kind of danger and excitement in their work. Most people found their niches in the Service. Some were after the prestige of presidential protection, while others worried that the demands of that kind of detail would interfere with their family life. Some wanted a more stable nine-to-five headquarters job, while others, like me, did not care what hours we worked. I just wanted the experience, the opportunities, the excitement, and the adrenaline.

I took my time typing my report, and when I was done, I casually got up from my desk and headed over to counterfeiting. When I knocked on his open door, Malfi lifted his head from some paperwork and raised his sunken eyes.

"You wanted to see me, sir?"

I couldn't be sure, but I think the tilt of his head and his lips tightening under his Pacino-in-*Serpico* mustache were what passed for a smile.

"Yeah. Good news, Mar"—in his New York accent, he pronounced my name like it rhymed with "there," as if we were good friends (I do not like people calling me Mary or Mar, but Malfi could get away with it)—"I finally got approval for you to help us out. You're still assigned to check forgery, but you'll join my squad when we need you. Raids, interviews, whatever comes up. You'll have to report for squad meetings and briefings, too. You know the deal."

Raids? Suspect interviews? Briefings? Finally, I was going to get to dip my toes into the exciting stuff. For a split second, I thought about the advice from other agents, who had said that, as a new agent, it was probably better to stick to my cases and avoid situations where I could get shot. That might work for them, but let's be honest, I joined the USSS for some adrenaline chasing. And this opportunity felt golden. It felt bold. It felt right. I looked back at Ron Malfi, reminding myself to keep breathing, and did my best to refrain from raising my eyebrows and widening my eyes.

"Yes, sir. Thank you, sir."

As I left his office and headed back to my desk, I stopped holding back. I squeezed my fist and let out a big grin—just for a second. YES! Raids! Finally. Fucking A!

• • •

Less than one week later, I was sitting at my desk in check forgery, looking at my case files and figuring out which ones I wanted to work that day, when I heard that unmistakable voice. "Mar, let's go." I looked up and saw Ron Malfi walking toward my desk. "We're meeting in the squad room. You're on." Holy shit, it was really happening. I closed my files, put them away, let my ATSAIC know where I was heading, and joined the counterfeiting team in their squad room.

"Everyone, you all know Agent Wilkas. She will be joining us on this case from soup to nuts." The team welcomed me warmly. A female agent had saved a seat for me next to her. Things were off to a good start.

Malfi, whom I now called "Boss," began the meeting. "OK. We have a lead on a perp: Carlos Rincon. He's been a person of interest for about a year, but we haven't been able to get any solid leads to make it worth our while—until now."

He continued. "We've had several arrests for people passing counterfeit from what we've deduced to be the same source, and in interviews our boy Carlos was named as the source by four of them." *Jackpot.* "So, ladies and gentlemen, you all know how this works—we have a case to build." There were smiles all around the table and an energy that was palpable.

As with other law enforcement agencies, in the Secret Service, if you don't build an airtight case, you will not get the district attorney's office to work with you to get a judge to grant you a warrant. Bring a shit case too many times, word gets around, and you will find it very difficult to get any of the assistant district attorneys to ever work with you. Here's the other thing: if you spend months on a case and you don't get a warrant, you don't nail the mope, you don't clear the case. And that means you have hell to pay. Not only was USSS headquarters lax in ever acknowledging when we did do good work, we were always being compared with the New York Field Office. We were like the ugly stepsister, never quite measuring up because the NYC office cleared more cases—and higher profile ones at that.

Building a case takes time. A lot of it. And investigative time competes with protection assignment time, so the balance was tricky. Counterfeit investigations are all-encompassing. Agents spend days, weeks, even months sometimes following the target and sitting on his house to establish his routine, who else might be living in the house, who all is involved—anything and everything we can determine. The more solid information we collect, the better, not just for the warrant but also for a kick-ass, well-executed raid. With Rincon, that's exactly what we did—we spent time, the endless hours needed, gathering more than enough incriminating intelligence to get a warrant for the perp's house.

The profile for our target was as follows: Carlos Rincon, Colombian male, twenty-five years old, living with his parents who didn't speak English. His priors were petty offenses, no felonies. In addition to Carlos and his parents, eight other individuals were living in the home in Southeast DC, all of them Hispanic: two brothers, three friends, one of the friend's girlfriend, and two toddlers. All were illegal immigrants, except for the two toddlers—they had been born in the US.

There was a rap on the conference room table as somebody put their empty coffee mug down, hard. A younger agent in the corner was sitting backwards on his chair and rubbing his foot back and forth in the brown carpet. For what felt like the hundredth time, Malfi turned to me and asked, "OK, Wilkas, walk me through your duties."

We were all sitting in the counterfeiting squad's conference room, waiting to head out and execute the warrant on Rincon. There were maybe eight agents there, most of them pretty seasoned, most of them men. Malfi's first order of business had been to make sure everybody was present and ready before he started assigning who would be where, doing what, with whom, when, and so on during the operation. But even now, with the briefing finished and the team just about ready to launch, I could see his eyes going around the room, from agent to agent, evaluating how prepared each of us was. He went over the scenario again. It was almost 2:00 a.m.

It was common for raids to happen in the early hours of the morning for the element of surprise. The mopes were notorious for partying all night, so they usually slept until noon. We were expected to be rested up, ready. Malfi had a reputation for being street-smart, but not sloppy. I'd heard of people being sent home for not being with it during a preraid briefing. I understood that. If you couldn't be on your toes in a briefing, what would happen out in the street? I certainly wasn't going to show up looking like shit, sucking down coffee, unprepared.

"I'm in the second wave," I began. I wasn't one of the lead agents—the first two agents to enter the target location, standing right at the front door. I would be just behind them. Although I was a young agent and this was my first raid, I was the only team member that spoke Spanish, so they needed me right upon entry into Rincon's house.

There were always two agents right on the front door. Sometimes you knock and the door is answered, sometimes you might have to breach the door—that's what we had the warrant for. There would be people stacked, one after the other, on the right and left sides of the door. There would be people in the back of the house too. If anybody tried to be clever and escape out the back, agents would be there to stop them.

"Mar." The boss pointed at me, pursed his lips, tugged at his mustache. "What if it all goes great and they answer the door and they're like, 'OK, I'm busted.' What do we do then?"

"Sir, we've got to see who else is in the house. We know there are eleven people living there, but we don't know who else might be there for the night. We can't assume shit—I mean anything—sir."

"OK, so we breach. Mar, where are you?"

Malfi wasn't picking on me; he went around the whole room, agent by agent, making sure every agent knew exactly what the plan was and what role they played in that plan. We went over it again. All of us. Who was going to drive over with whom. Where everyone was going to be before we knocked on the door. Where everyone was going to be when we were actually knocking on the door. Who was going to breach the door if they didn't answer. And on and on.

Even the veteran agents went over their duties for the umpteenth time. How many times had they sat in this conference room like this? I realized that we were telling each other just as much as we were answering the boss. I knew what I was supposed to do. I knew what everybody else was supposed to do. And by the end of the briefing, each of us knew that the others knew what to do. We also knew it could all go to shit and all of our planning would go out the window. Plan for the worst, hope for the best, as we said. Before we walked out of the conference room to get our gear, we were a team. We were sure of the other agents we were heading out with, and we felt responsible for each other and our mission.

"Let's remember we chose this time because, from our surveillance, we know his schedule—when he works, when he shits, when he eats, and when he sleeps. We know when we go in"—Ron looked at his watch—"in one hour, that he's been home with lights out, already asleep for just over an hour."

We knew this because two of our team members were sitting on the house. You don't do all that work to build a case and then fuck it up by just assuming the shitbird is going to cooperate on the night you are raiding his house. You want confirmation.

We went over the neighborhood, the address, the block, the house. We reviewed every detail we had. The raid would start on a stoop at a house in Southeast DC. It was the kind of neighborhood where, if I were walking around in broad daylight, I'd notice lots of people looking at me. A lot of guys hanging and watching. I'd think, *Is my vehicle gonna be there when I get back?* I might hear someone on the street say, "Oh no, it's the big 5-0"—like it was some kind of public announcement. Would my parents end up reading about me in the nightly news?

But it would be 3:00 a.m. when we went in, and our team was carrying so much firepower, nobody was going to call us out on the street. Still, we *really* didn't know what we'd walk into in that house. You never do. Most of the time, we didn't get shot at or find weapons on anybody, but you just didn't know. Prepare for the worst. . . . The adrenaline was pumping through my veins, and the feeling was the same. Would I make it home?

Damn right I would.

The first wave of agents were typically the bigger, more intimidating agents. I was in the second wave because I was needed to communicate with the people inside in Spanish. We were all lined up, stacked, on the stoop when we got the go-ahead for the two lead agents to knock on the door, to bust it down if no one responded after two attempts. That wouldn't be necessary that night. After the first agent knocked, we all watched as the door creaked part of the way open. It had been left ajar. One of the Colombians must have been partying too hard to remember to lock up.

"Federal agents. We have a warrant," the lead agent called out. Crickets. The sound of the door bouncing open on its hinges again was the only response to the lead agent's second knock.

Once the first wave of agents was in, I followed. Again, "Federal Agents. We have a warrant." The moment we were inside, we heard voices, chaos, everywhere in the house. We knew the layout of the place—we'd been looking at it all night in the conference room. Since there was no one with whom I immediately needed to communicate with in Spanish, I was responsible for clearing rooms, with one agent in front of me and one behind me, starting with the first room on the left. We went room to room, calling out what we saw.

"Clear!"

In the back of my mind, I was praying I didn't get blown away from behind, because my focus was forward and on the room to the left, one other agent in front of me. I wouldn't be pointing my weapon at him, but I had it out, essentially pointed at the floor, ready to go, and I was slightly crouched. I had to really trust the agent behind me since I was focused left, right, and forward, and not on my six.

"Get out of bed! Put your hands up."

The parents were the first people we encountered. The mother screamed her head off when she woke to a hulking agent with a gun in his hand in her bedroom. I stepped forward and, in Spanish, told her, "Federal agents. We have a warrant." I used short commands, "Stop screaming, señora. Please. We are not here to hurt you. Please calm down, señora." She grabbed her husband, asking him what was going on. He was calm but confused, doing his best to comfort his wife while federal agents spread out through the rooms rounding up their occupants.

From the room I checked, I called out, "We need another agent in here. There are two unsubs [unidentified subjects] in here." We brought them to the room where we were holding everyone else and finally got word that the whole house was clear.

Our perp, his brother, the three friends, and the girlfriend had all been sound asleep. Thank God for small favors. And there were no "extra" surprises or straphangers for the evening. Once the house was cleared, two agents took Carlos to WFO to interview him. We didn't know if he spoke English or not. I stayed at the house until we were done there. We collected IDs from everyone, interviewed each of them, ran checks on them, and determined who else might be involved and needed to come down to WFO to join Carlos. We encouraged them to talk with us and give accurate information—or else INS might need to be informed that most of them were here illegally.

Along with another agent, I escorted Carlos's brother, his hands restrained in the front of his body by flexicuffs, to one of the bedrooms, where he claimed his ID was. Once we were there, he walked to his dresser and started to open a drawer.

"STOP!" I called out.

"But my ID is in this drawer," he said, acting a little too innocent.

"I'll get it. You walk over to him." I pointed to the agent at my side and went to the dresser myself. When I opened the drawer, his ID was, indeed, there. So was a shiny new revolver. Loaded. Asshole.

"What's this?" I asked.

"Oh, that? For protection only," he said, like it was no big deal. "DC is a dangerous place. You know how it is." I sure do, asshole.

Of course, when we called it in, the weapon came up as unregistered. The brother would join Carlos down at WFO when we finished our interviews and our search of the house. We took our time, doing our best to figure out who else might be involved in the counterfeiting operation. The parents seemed genuinely shocked that their Carlos could be involved in anything illegal. After all, they raised him better than that, a good Catholic boy.

Were the parents a danger? The brother? What about the three friends and the girlfriend? Were any of them co-conspirators? Was there more going on than we knew? If you make the wrong presumption in a situation like this, you and your whole team can get whacked, ending up as the top story on the day's news. Human beings are not predictable, particularly when they are caught off guard, half asleep, during a raid in the middle of the night, and you don't *really* know who all is involved. Did I ever have people that resisted my commands? Did I have people that acted like they didn't understand English or my Spanish? Did I have to fight to get people to the ground? Yes, yes, and yes. Was it to the point where I feared for my life? Absolutely. But my instinct for survival was strong.

About two weeks later, back at WFO, Malfi called to me from his office. "Mar, come here a minute."

Yes, sir. As I sat in the chair in front of his desk, he asked me how I felt about working undercover. "Talk to me," I said, calm and cool on the outside while my adrenaline began to spike on the inside.

Malfi laughed. He then told me they were investigating an individual who had a business that was believed to be a cover for manufacturing false US passports for Spanish-speaking individuals. The counterfeiting squad wanted to bust open his operation. My role was to go into his storefront in Arlington, ask for a particular individual, and play the part of a South American damsel in distress and in desperate need of a US passport. All I had to do was get him to commit to making me that false passport.

This was an incredible, rare opportunity. Undercover operations in the USSS are uncommon. It's just not how the Service typically works. But personally, it was a dream assignment. I jumped at the chance to get in the thick of things.

I had just one hesitation, which I did not share with anyone: I'm bilingual, but even in Spain, where I learned the language, they can tell I have an accent. An American accent. *Gringa*, they used to say. That was something that could raise an eyebrow for a Latino guy running a US passport-forging operation in DC. Where was I supposed to be from?

What the hell, I thought, *I'll figure all of that out.* Besides, I was the only Spanish speaker in the Washington Field Office. Who else were they gonna use? I was a new agent being handed an insanely cool mission by a superior, a guy I revered. I didn't ask a lot of questions or raise objections. The Service had a lead on a case they'd worked hard to develop, and it seemed like I was their best shot at carrying it out. I wasn't going to turn them down.

A few days later, I was fully briefed, set up with a wire, and handed a panic button to keep in my pocket. Just in case. The window of the storefront was plastered with so many brightly colored signs and fliers offering everything from money orders and check cashing to fax services and discounted international phone cards that you could hardly make out what was going on inside from the street. I walked in, hyperalert, blood pumping. I didn't show how nervous I was. I smiled humbly, said hello, and did my best to express to the proprietor—in Spanish—how desperate I was for a US passport.

"I can't help you here," he said, his voice stern.

He wasn't buying my act. Did he know I was a Fed trying to bust his operation? I hadn't asked many questions about the assignment because I hadn't wanted to seem hesitant or scared. Now I realized how little I knew. Was there a part of the story I hadn't gotten? If I pushed further, would this guy pull a knife? A gun? One way to find out.

I had that panic button in my pocket if I needed it and a safe word too. There was a team in a car only a half block up the road listening in on the wire, and I knew that if I gave the word they'd be on their way. False sense of security? Possibly. But I was thinking to myself, *Welcome to the big leagues, Wilkas. Toughen up.* Besides, even pushing that button was a risk: I'd have to stick one of my hands into my pocket to use it, thus lessening my ability to defend myself. Better to keep my hands free in case he tried to do anything. (Old habits die hard: I still have a hard time putting my hands in my pockets.)

I did not give up. I tried from another angle—flattery. I told him that he came very highly recommended and that I had been told he was the person that could help me. Again I heard, "I can't help you here." I took a deep breath, not losing eye contact with him, and tried again from yet another angle, the desperately begging angle. I got the same answer for a third and fourth time. I asked if he knew anyone who might be able to help me. He simply shook his head no.

I realized that no matter how I prodded or pleaded, my accent had likely betrayed me, or he'd otherwise nailed me as a Fed. I uttered a defeated, "Gracias, señor. Adios," and with one eye trained on the guy,

I slowly left the store, adrenaline still going full blast. I then walked to the meeting point, got in the car with the other agents, and exhaled.

We debriefed the entire ride back to WFO. "You did great, Mar. Man, you are tenacious." I smiled, but I was beyond disappointed. I wanted to take this business and this guy down. "We knew it was less than a 50/50 shot with this guy, but it was worth trying. Thanks for having the guts to take this on." I'd hoped this mission would be the one that got me permanently assigned to the counterfeit squad. But, unfortunately, no such luck.

The pressure, other agents, danger, the routine—things that were difficult at first started to become second nature to me. I started feeling more confident in my skills as a USSS Agent.

The other rookies and I had done a lot of foreign dignitary command post assignments. A senior agent would always be there, and the new agents would learn how to set up command posts, which involved putting up cameras and getting the communications system going. We'd have maps, our protectees' schedules, batteries charging for the radios, extra radios, and phones. The command post was considered a down room as well, so it would typically be stocked with food, drinks, and a place to rest. Downtime was essential for keeping agents alert. I was starting to feel like I had the process of setting up command posts down pat.

I learned how to better deal with static posts too. As a rookie agent, my concern was, "What can I do to stay alert for as long as possible? How long can I watch this door or elevator or hallway and not nod off?" As time went on and I completed more missions and stood more posts, I learned some tricks. I had to.

The details of how a static post is run is partially up to the shift leader, and it can be a tough juggling act for them. They may only be given, say, twenty agents to work a site when the optimal situation would be to have thirty. So, what can the shift leader do to make sure everyone stays on their toes? Well, two things: one, rotate people—because even a new door is a change of scenery, a new scenario, and some physical movement—and, two, check-in. "Wilkas, how you doing? You need a push?"—meaning, do you need to go to the bathroom? You need someone to come and relieve your post, give you some downtime? You need something to eat? It was surprising how much even the most minimal communication can keep an agent alert. There was, however, never idle chatter because those lines of communication had to stay clear in case anything important went down.

I learned, too, that my post might be to watch a particular door, but my responsibilities included everything and everyone within my field of vision. This same "rule" also held when I later worked VIPs in the first concentric ring of security.

If I was working a detail in a building with a pretty massive crowd, there were things that became innate. While within arm's reach of the protectee, I could spot somebody who looked nervous. Why was that guy keeping his hands in his pockets? Why did he keep looking around? I'd radio it in. "At my three o'clock, white guy, older, grungy looking, green trench coat, twitchy, worth a visit."

In a situation like that, I might have been unsure of myself early on. Was I making the right call? Was I really seeing what I thought I was? At campaign events, there were huge crowds. They were always so intimidating. As a rookie, you didn't want to be that agent that calls out every person, but you knew you couldn't neglect to call out a threat either. Later on, I just dealt with it and moved on.

And then I was back to scanning from person to person in the crowd. The VIP was shaking hands—everybody's hands—so I was a bobblehead, looking at each person's hands, taking mental notes. There was the VIP. There were two agents on one side of him, and two on the other. We had an agent behind us as well. Another agent—a floater, who went where they were needed—was within eyeshot of the VIP. And, of course, we had an agent in the crowd, sometimes more. A voice came over the radio: "Let's make it a tighter circle." There were four, five, sometimes six of us, depending on the protectee. We closed up, and we were like a set of human surveillance cameras, each with our own field of view, overlapping but spread out. We were each doing our part and confident that everyone else was doing theirs in order to accomplish our primary objective: keep the VIP safe, no matter what.

At first, this can be overwhelming. As a rookie, I didn't always know exactly where to look. The VIP just shook that skinny guy's hand, then a brown-haired guy, a tall female; he moved on; now he was going to cross the aisle and shake the next hand, kiss the next baby.

How was the VIP doing? The rookie agent might look at him, try to assess whether everything was going OK, what his next move might be.

But the VIP is the one person in this room I know is not a threat. That guy whose hand was shaken three seconds ago? He's in my field of view now, and I'm keeping my eye on him until the agent who's to my left or right can see him. Just because the VIP has already shaken the guy's hand doesn't mean that he isn't a threat, that he couldn't pull a weapon out at any time. Hell no. That would be a perfect time to make an attempt to hurt the VIP—when he's passed, and you think the agents have their attention elsewhere. The VIP's six, or backside, is actually a key position, and it's often overlooked by inexperienced protection teams. (When Yitzhak Rabin's team overlooked it, Rabin's assassin walked right up behind him and shot him in the back of the head.)

If I was covering the VIP's six, sometimes I'd walk backwards while still keeping up with the flow of the VIP's movements. I might bump into somebody. I might be focusing on someone or something and realize the VIP and the team had moved on. It was all a learning process. It took a while, but eventually I figured it out. As an agent, regardless of my post, I was able to get myself to the point where I could take myself out of the moment and focus—not on tedium or what the VIP was doing, whether it was the president, the first lady, or another protectee; not on worries about what might happen; not on how to avoid embarrassing myself or whether another agent thought I belonged in the Secret Service or not; but, rather, on my duties. I knew where to look, I understood why, and I finally . . . well, I finally felt like I belonged.

But even a confident agent can face obstacles.

I was still honing my skills on that late January morning when I got the call from Special Agent in Charge Basham while on my detail protecting the Bush grandchildren. I had been learning as much as I could about protection, about investigations, about hierarchy, about office politics. But what did I know about Internal Affairs (IA) investigations? I knew squat. Internal Affairs was for people who screwed up, not me.

The following Monday morning, February 4, at 9:00 a.m. sharp, I knocked on SAIC Basham's door. He greeted me with a smile and told me to come in and close the door.

Shit.

CHAPTER
3

WASHINGTON, DC

1992

SAIC Basham removed his glasses and closed the file folder he was reading as I shut the door behind me. I spotted my name on the folder before he turned it face down on his desk and looked up at me, a friendly expression in his eyes.

"Have a seat, Mary Beth."

He was extremely calm, but SAIC Basham was always extremely calm. He began by telling me, once again, that he did not think the issue with IA was a big deal. Then, he described to me how the flow of information is supposed to work with USSS Special Agent candidates.

"Once a candidate has reached the point in the hiring process where the USSS has begun the background investigation, the Service sends out inquiries to other relevant federal agencies—the IRS, DEA, FBI, etc.—asking whether any of those agencies has any information or a file on the candidate." Back in February 1991, SAIC Basham said, that is exactly what the USSS did for me. Because they never received any significant information on me, they moved forward and offered me employment. However, almost an entire year later, after I'd already become an established agent, one agency did, finally, respond: the FBI. And the information they responded with was why I was in the SAIC's office that morning.

"Now," SAIC Basham told me, "Internal Affairs has contacted me. They want to speak with you, Mary Beth. When I asked for more specifics, all they told me was it had to do with your FBI application."

He didn't ask me for any details or explanations. He simply let me know that I would be meeting with IA at the headquarters building after lunch.

"OK, sir."

"Mary Beth, you've done an outstanding job for the Service thus far, and you are one of the most promising new agents we've had." He replaced his glasses, and a closed-mouth smile wrinkled his face. "I really don't think this is a big deal." The SAIC had a stellar reputation, not just for being calm but for being eminently reasonable and solid. If he didn't think I should worry, then maybe I didn't need to. But let's be honest, this was IA, not a reprimand for spending too much time in the gym.

After leaving SAIC Basham's office, I checked my mailbox. No protection assignments today. In hindsight, I am certain that was prearranged. I headed to my desk and stared blankly at the stack of investigation files waiting to be closed out. I knew I should get to work and make good use of this time, but my mind was elsewhere. Then the phone rang. I was being called into the office of my direct supervisor, Giles Coffey. When I got there, Agent Bill Clancy, ATSAIC and head of the check forgery squad in WFO, was also there. He also happened to be an attorney. Apparently they had both been informed of my "situation." Giles asked if I wanted to go to my IA meeting that afternoon with Bill Clancy as my attorney. Bill said, "You have the right to legal representation, and it's probably a good idea."

I thought about it for a bit but I turned him down. As SAIC Basham had said, the meeting with IA probably wouldn't be a big deal. Besides, if it was, would it make any difference if I had a lawyer there? To this day, I really don't know whether I made the right decision. Probably not.

That afternoon, I sat in a small conference room in a less-than-comfortable chair. Somehow what was happening didn't feel quite real.

"Thanks again for coming down, Mary Beth," the first IA agent said. His partner didn't say anything. He just stared right at me, his hand holding his chin and covering his mouth as he sat back.

Then, he lurched forward, both hands gripping the table. He blurted out, "We know about the arrest!"

I had never been arrested in my life, so I told him I had no idea what he was talking about. This was followed by accusations of me lying and "covering up the crime, arrest, and incarceration."

Then the first agent put a hand on his partner's shoulder, as if he were restraining him. In a gentle voice, he told me, "Look, Mary Beth, we're here to help you. We just want to resolve this issue and move on."

I didn't know Scamp and Striver, the two IA investigators interviewing me, but they looked like the guys that I worked with every day in the field, which is what they were after all. Internal Affairs was a rotation in the USSS, a position you applied for and filled for a few years. On another day, these two agents could have been my colleagues, friends even. But on this day, they were playing out a good cop/bad cop performance that was like something from a cheesy TV show.

I got it. They were doing their jobs. I understood that the Secret Service had a right to clarify the "discrepancies" they felt they had found in my background. However, what was going on here was tremendously bad form. In Interviewing 101, as I call it, I'd learned that you adapt your tactics to the situation and responses of the subject: your tactics should match the goal. You can always escalate, make your style and demeanor more aggressive, but once you engage in accusation, condescension, and other negative tactics, you will rarely be able to de-escalate. Did I expect IA to treat me nicely? Actually, yes. I expected to be treated as a fellow agent, not like I was some criminal pulled off the streets of DC and interrogated with immediate disdain, mistrust, and arrogance.

It was clear to me that these two IA agents were not looking to clear up any misunderstanding. Nope. They had their minds made up—I was guilty—and they were not going to back down. They were so clearly determined to make this a bigger case than it was that they scraped up a ridiculous and minor incident that occurred during my freshman year of college, calling it an arrest and incarceration, and attempted to make it seem like a major cover-up of a scandal from my past.

The Secret Service was "investigating" whether I had specifically obfuscated two items from my past during my USSS application: The first was my admitted hashish use while I was in Spain. The second—the purported "arrest"—is what I'll call "the case of the malted milk eggs." When I was a freshman at Indiana University, I was shopping in a grocery store in town with a friend of mine, Suzanne. We had coordinated a social event (read: party) in our dorm and tasked ourselves with the shopping. It was around Easter, and, as such, the store had a huge display of Easter decorations and candy at its entrance. Suzanne and I found when we first entered the grocery store that we both had a love for malted milk balls, which, during Easter, came in the form of malted milk Easter eggs. We picked up a bag, opened it, and put it in our cart to nibble on while we were shopping. As we were going up and down the aisles shopping, checking off all of the items on our list, we were in malted milk egg heaven. Suffice it to say that we had no problem polishing off the entire bag during our grocery shopping extravaganza.

After we paid for our groceries, we walked outside the store and waited for a taxi back to campus. A tall, stern-looking man walked up to us and said, "Hello. Did you girls forget to pay for something inside the store?" Suzanne and I looked at each other. Neither of us had any idea what he was talking about, so we responded, "Um. No." He then told us he was an undercover security guard and had observed us eating a bag of malted milk eggs for which we had not paid. "Oh my gosh!" Suzanne and I instantly realized. We told him we were really sorry and would head back in and pay for the candy. Mr. Undercover told us, "Sorry, it's too late. You already left the store without paying for the candy. Please come with me."

We followed him to the store manager's office where he and the store manager accused us of shoplifting, of purposely not paying for the bag of malted milk eggs. We insisted that it was not intentional, that we simply left the empty bag in the cart. The store manager acted like we had committed a felony. I looked at the store manager and told him that I was a criminal justice major at IU and would not risk my future career on a stupid bag of malted milk eggs. He laughed and said, "Well, you should have thought of that before you shoplifted." What? I then said, "Why would we pay for an entire cart full of groceries and NOT pay for a seventy-nine-cent bag of candy?" His answer: "Because you are two arrogant kids from IU who think you can do whatever you want in this town and get away with it." Wow.

There were no police involved. There was no arrest. But they told us they were going to pursue this in court because they wanted us to "pay for our misdeed and to make an example of us." Unbelievable. Suzanne and I really had no choice but to share this not-so-great-news with our parents who, subsequently, helped us hire an attorney. After two meetings with our lawyer and a court appearance the following fall in Bloomington, we were sentenced to thirty hours of community service for the class A misdemeanor of "conversion," a fancy way of saying "petty theft" or "shoplifting." Per the judge and state's attorney's agreement, there was to be no record of the incident once all of the judge's requirements were met. In other words, provided we did our community service and stayed out of trouble for a year, our records would be expunged, wiped out, nonexistent.

Although the entire situation had been a total pain in the ass and pretty embarrassing, I actually enjoyed doing community service, and I met some pretty nice people. I started the first Saturday after my "sentencing" and worked a bunch of Saturdays in a row, cleaning up trash on the highway around Bloomington. Then, on September 3, 1985, with all of the judge's items checked off the list, I applied for earned dismissal by the court and, on April 8, 1986, my application was accepted and my record was expunged.

IA Inspectors Scamp and Striver spent hours accusing me of premeditated lying on my Secret Service application, falsifying specific questions on my application, lying during the polygraph, getting away with deceit during the polygraph, and covering up my past "arrest and incarceration" at Indiana University. Our session ended with me spending forty-five minutes or so writing a nine-page statement articulating my explanation of each of the two allegations. The final sentence on that nine-page statement was, "If necessary, I am willing to take another polygraph examination to clear up any doubts regarding these incidents."

At the beginning of the interview, I had been clinging to hope that, as the SAIC had said, this would be "no big deal." Five minutes in, I was shocked and pissed off. By the time I left, five long hours later, I was sure that my career in the USSS would soon be over.

The sky had been bright and clear when I had gone into the headquarters building. Now, the brisk winter evening was dark as I walked into the mostly empty Washington Field Office well past 5 p.m. I was glad it was quiet; no one was there to look up from their desk and wonder where I was coming in from. My mailbox was still empty, so I headed back to my desk to collect my things before heading home.

To my surprise, the SAIC was waiting for me there. He stood with his hands in his pockets and no sign of impatience on his face—I couldn't tell if he'd been waiting for a minute or an hour.

"Mary Beth." He nodded toward his office and I followed him. "How did it go?"

He was none too happy to learn that IA had interviewed me for so long. In fact, as I continued to debrief him, a brief twitch of anger crossed his face, a rarity for the rock-steady SAIC.

"They had no right to keep you that long. They lied to me. They said they were only going to ask you a few questions!"

The phone rang, and when SAIC Basham answered it, I got up from my chair to make my way to the door, thinking he would want privacy for the call.

"Yes, of course. I understand."

SAIC Basham raised his hand to me and lifted a finger, essentially telling me not to leave. I complied, and quietly sat back down as he finished up his call. As he hung up the phone, I saw another brief flicker—Surprise? Confusion? Anger?—cross his face before he turned to me. Once again, he was impassive, composed. His face and body language gave away nothing.

"Mary Beth, that was Agent Striver. IA has requested to see you again first thing tomorrow morning."

"OK, sir."

"He said they just want to clarify one last issue. I'm sure it's no big deal."

"Yes, sir."

"Listen, Mary Beth. You're an excellent agent, one of the best new agents we've had in a while. This should not be a big deal."

That meant a lot. SAIC Basham's opinion, as the head of the WFO and as an agent with a stellar reputation, was worth a tremendous amount to me.

"Get a good night's sleep and know that we'll do whatever it takes to get you through this. This whole thing won't be a problem at all. It's nothing."

"Thank you, sir."

I trusted and respected SAIC Basham, and I wanted to believe what he said. As I turned and left his office, I was glad that he couldn't see the worry on my face. I knew it wasn't "nothing"; after all, I was the one who had just been grilled for five hours by IA. I knew how they were handling this investigation. I knew how they had treated me. And when they called me back for another visit—I mean another "interview"—the next morning, I knew I was screwed.

On February 5, 1992, at 8:30 a.m., I once again reported for an interview with IA Inspectors Scamp and Striver. The night before, I had fantasized about them calling me in and saying, "Based on our interview of yesterday and our Internal Affairs investigation, your case has been dismissed in your favor," then apologizing for treating me like shit. But, in the cold light of morning, I knew that was wishful thinking. Based on what had happened the day before, I was pretty sure I was well on my way out; it was simply a question of time. What I didn't know was the nature of the "one last issue" that had to be cleared up.

It was a beaut.

The IA inspectors "believed" I had been deceitful when I answered "No" to question 26 on the SF 86: "Has the United States Government ever investigated your background?"

I closed my eyes.

"YOU HAVE GOT TO BE FUCKING KIDDING ME!" This is exactly what I was screaming at them, only inside my head, not out loud. As much as I wanted to scream, that clearly would not have been prudent. I just sighed and let the interview proceed however it was going to. Protesting or saying anything besides direct answers to their questions would, in their minds, make me look guilty and desperate and would give them an advantage. So I simply listened and waited for the question.

After pausing for a minute or so after tossing that allegation my way, waiting for it to sink in, and hoping I would react, Scamp shared that IA felt the fact that I answered "No" to question 26 on my DEA application was deceitful. In other words, they believed that, because I had applied to the FBI in 1989 and to the DEA in 1991, I should have answered "Yes" to question 26—"Has the United States Government ever investigated your background?"—because, in their words, "clearly the government had investigated your background." But they didn't just come out and say this; we had to play their IA game again, and that meant spending a couple more hours together—me in the hot seat, them messing with me, thinking they were going to get me to confess my sins.

"Of course, you had to know the FBI had investigated you."

Except that we all knew that is not how the government application process works. As I explained to the boys across the table, my application with the FBI never got to the background-investigation stage.

Scamp continued to badger me, saying, "Come on, Mary Beth, don't you think you should have answered 'Yes' to question 26? I mean, are you telling me that you don't think the FBI looked even a little bit into your background?"

My response: "No, Inspector, I don't. The FBI rejected my application. Why would they waste the time and money looking into my background?"

I thought that would be the end of it and I would write yet another statement and be done. Instead, there was a little pause in the room. I knew this tactic. It meant Inspectors Scamp and Striver were not done.

Striver said to me, "Mary Beth, you filled out an SF 86 as part of the application process to become a Special Agent with the DEA and signed it on August 23, 1990. You had to have known they were looking into your background by the time you signed the SF 86 on January 23, 1991, for the USSS."

It took me a minute to sort through the dates in my head, but I knew the facts of my application process, inside and out. I responded, "Although I did, in fact, sign an SF 86 as part of the process to become a Special Agent with the DEA on August 23, 1990, there was a delay in processing my application." They asked me to explain. Of course, my pleasure, boys. Long story short, when I moved from Chicago to Washington, DC, shortly after returning from Spain, it took several months to get my DEA file forwarded from the Chicago Field Office to their DC office. Therefore, there was a lengthy delay in my application. In other words, no background investigation had begun with the DEA before April 12, 1991, and, therefore, no, I was not deceitful when I answered "No" to question 26 on my USSS SF 86 and signed the form on January 23, 1991.

Silence. Here's the thing—they knew ALL of this. They had every single document from both my FBI and my DEA applications. They had spoken with people from both agencies.

After two more hours of being badgered, I wrote yet another statement about this new allegation, but this time it was only one paragraph long.

After the second IA interview, I debriefed the SAIC again. Then, for a long time, nothing happened. Well, I didn't directly hear a word about what was happening with my case, although I am certain there was plenty happening over at IA. I was back to my desk, back to investigations, back to protection assignments, and back to work. Weeks passed, and nobody in the field office besides my supervisors (and their supervisors) even knew that anything was going on, which is how I wanted it. I didn't want to discuss it with anyone; I just wanted to continue with my duties as if nothing had changed.

But a lot had changed. I was convinced my career with the USSS was over, yet I continued to be given protection assignments every day and to work on my investigations as usual. Meanwhile, in another building down the road, the USSS was still scrambling to find whatever they could to mount their case against me. I was under scrutiny and under investigation by the agency I was working for. I knew it was for some bullshit reasons, but I knew that somewhere up the chain of command, something wasn't right.

The USSS clearly had nothing substantial with which to let me go from employment as a Special Agent, just a judgment call as to whether or not I was telling the truth as to how I filled out the SF 86 and SF 86A. I found myself constantly going back and forth between worry and confidence. When I left my desk each evening, I didn't know if I'd be back in the morning. There were days when I repeated to myself what SAIC Basham had told me several times—"This isn't going to be an issue." And there were days when I believed it, but they were few and far between.

Eventually SAIC Basham got promoted, and he was no longer part of the WFO. The former Assistant Special Agent in Charge, Joe Domingo, was now the SAIC. On May 14, 1992, he called me into his office.

When I walked into SAIC Domingo's office, the new ASAIC, Tommy Castile, was also there. They both sat down, and Domingo asked me to take a seat. SAIC Domingo looked at me and hesitated. Then, there it was, my worst fear being uttered from his mouth.

"Mary, the Secret Service has decided not to continue your employment. Your contract will not be renewed as of May 30." He then added, "Campania made the decision," referring to Deputy Director Guido Campania. Wow, it was really happening. As of May 30, 1992, I was no longer going to be a United States Secret Service agent.

I waited for a few seconds, but nothing else was said. "OK,

Mr. Domingo," I said. "Thank you. Is there anything else I need to know?"

SAIC Domingo didn't answer. He just sat there looking at me, dumbfounded, waiting for a reaction from me, I suspect. After about a minute, likely wondering if I truly understood his message, he felt obligated to repeat the punch line: "Mary, the Secret Service is letting you go as of the end of this month. They will not be renewing your employment contract." No doubt he thought I was going to break down in one form or another—cry, plead, beg—I don't know. No fucking way. I told him I understood. I thanked him again and was about to get up and leave his office when ASAIC Castile spoke up.

"Mary Beth," he started as he leaned forward in his chair, looking me right in the eye. With a broad smile on his face, he said, "I highly encourage you to pursue the EEO route."

I had no idea what he meant. At the time, I did not even know what EEO meant, but SAIC Domingo's head had snapped to ASAIC Castile on hearing the words, and he looked none too happy, so I made sure to file that little tidbit away to look into later. Domingo rose from his seat then.

"OK, Mary. If you have any questions, I'll be here. It's been great working with you."

I had just over two more weeks with the USSS. That afternoon, I had a protection assignment to get to. When I returned from it, I found a handwritten note on my desk. It was from ASAIC Tommy Castile: "Please see me later today."

Thankfully, I had done a quick check in my training manuals before I headed out for my protection assignment. I quickly found out what EEO—Equal Employment Opportunity—was and realized that it was meant to protect employees from discrimination in the workplace.

When I knocked on ASAIC Castile's door, he was clearly pleased I had decided to hear him out. He walked over to shake my hand and sat next to me on the far side of his desk. He strongly recommended I file an EEO suit against the Service for discrimination based on sex.

"I don't want to get into specifics, but I've had a tussle with the USSS myself, Mary Beth. I did whatever it took to win it, and I'm glad I did."

Wow. I didn't expect such openness from the ASAIC. I still hadn't talked about my issues with anyone outside or inside the Service, not even my parents.

He continued. "Do yourself a favor and look into a variety of cases. There are some that will definitely help yours. Agents have been busted with drugs while on the job, failed their polygraphs on drug questions, and been arrested for DUI, assault, and burglary, and are still on the job."

Now I was in shock—not only because these cases allegedly existed within the USSS but also because ASAIC Castile was telling me about them. I thanked ASAIC Castile and left his office with my head spinning, wanting to get everything he'd told me down on paper before I forgot any of the details.

A few days later, I received a letter in the mail signed by the assistant director of investigations, Randy Shafter, entitled "Expiration of Schedule B Appointment." It was essentially a form letter that reiterated that my schedule B appointment would expire on May 30, 1992. The letter also discussed the option of appealing via the Secret Service grievance procedure within fifteen days if I felt the decision was unjustified. In addition, the letter informed me that if I felt this action was being taken "based on discrimination due to race, color, religion, sex, age, handicap, or national origin" I could appeal through an Equal Employment Opportunity (EEO) counselor within thirty days.

In the weeks since I had first gotten the call about the IA investigation, I had gone from being a casual runner to becoming a long-distance runner. It had become my stress relief, my thinking time, my strength. Now, I filed the letter away in my room, and I changed into running clothes.

I still lived in Cleveland Park, in Northwest DC, just off the Metro's Red Line. The jog to Arlington National Cemetery through Rock Creek Park and back normally took me ninety minutes. I stepped out of my door and onto Connecticut Avenue, where I began running.

Had I been discriminated against? I wasn't sure. ASAIC Castile seemed to think that other agents—male agents—had done far worse without being reprimanded or terminated by the Service. Was it because they were men? Did the fact that I was a woman explain why the IA inspectors had treated me so harshly? I didn't think so. Scamp and Striver were definitely jackasses, but since my ordeal began, everyone I spoke with since then who had ever dealt with IA told me that it sucked and that "most IA agents forget where they came from and that they will eventually be back out in the field with us—the same colleagues they messed with." That seemed to just be the way IA did their job. And maybe the information ASAIC Castile had shared with me about other agents was true, but I knew nothing about the cases (or incidents) firsthand.

What I knew for sure was that I had the support of many of my male colleagues: SAIC Basham, my supervisors, other agents from WFO. Several had even called and come to visit me at home, asking about what had happened once they realized I was gone from WFO and not just out on a travel protection assignment. My experience in the Service certainly wasn't about male agents against the female agents.

The truth is, I just didn't know whether I fared better or worse in my IA investigation because I was a woman. One thing was for sure and was, I guess, potentially good for me: they were worried about a lawsuit. It was the kind of attention the USSS did not want. The USSS wanted—needed—more female agents. Besides, they had just invested a ton of money into my training, and since I was a new agent, I imagined that they didn't believe they had seen a return on their investment yet.

I had shaken my head in disbelief so many times during this investigation. I kept thinking, "You can't have it both ways." How could the agency consider me to be a top-notch candidate that became a well-liked, solid, and highly respected United States Secret Service agent and, at the same time, make me out to be a premeditated, scandalous double-crosser?

Suddenly—it felt like only moments since I'd begun running—I was crossing the cobblestone bridge over the Potomac and facing the high hedges that guard the monuments in Arlington National Cemetery. I could barely remember the route I'd taken to get there, just the stuff I'd wanted to process on the way—the USSS, the EEO, my career, my future. I saluted the entrance to the cemetery and turned around, ready to head home, looking forward to another head-clearing forty-five minutes.

CHAPTER
4

WASHINGTON, DC
1992

"Don't put that away too quickly. I'll be back," I said.

I had just handed over my gun to Renee Porter, WFO's office manager, who was also in charge of service equipment. She ticked off a box on her list and passed it back to me for my initials.

For a while, I hadn't been sure how I would play this game: should I fold and walk away, or should I double down and move forward, confident I had the edge? But now I was certain I had to fight to keep my position. To be honest, I didn't feel like I had any choice but to pursue this case, all the way to the end.

Why? For one, that's just who I am; I fight for what I believe in. I couldn't—I don't—just walk away, not from something I had worked so hard for, that felt so right, and that now, as a result of the Service's decision, felt so wrong and unjust. Also, to just let it go and move on seemed like I was admitting wrongdoing and playing into their bullshit game. The USSS's decision to not renew my employment contract was shortsighted, and I knew that the basis for the decision was not just misguided, it was full of holes. I also knew that precedent had been established by the Secret Service, and, while there were at least six male agents currently on the job who had allegedly been involved in illegal acts or had failed a polygraph exam, I was being let go for reasons that were still not quite clear: I had done nothing illegal.

I'd passed my polygraph, and after IA spent hours grilling me, they had come up with nothing that would justify letting me go as an agent.

Although I am not sure I would have articulated this at the time, as it was more of a subconscious motivator, I was also driven to pursue my case because I wanted to continue to be that anomaly—one of one hundred eighty women among two thousand US Secret Service agents. I had not just been a standout in training, I had become a well-respected and well-liked agent in just over one year on the job in the largest and most influential field office of the Secret Service. I wanted to continue to stand out—for the right reasons. I was angry, too. Obviously. The longer I contemplated my situation, the more I got pissed off at the injustice of what seemed like a contrived fiasco. If nothing else, I was not going to let the government intimidate me into backing down, crawling away, or giving up on myself or my dream. They might have been ready to dismiss this case, but I had to look myself in the mirror. So, in the end, the decision was easy. I was going to pursue this. I was going to see this through and do it with integrity, pride, and honor.

I turned over my handcuffs, radio, and the rest of my official gear. Renee ticked off the appropriate boxes. I initialed them.

"I'll be back," I said again.

Renee passed the form back to me for my signature and smiled.

"I hope so, Agent Wilkas," she said.

I knew—well, I'd been advised—that if I was going to fight the USSS over my job, I'd need an attorney—one with government experience. Peter Carre was referred to me by a friend in the Uniformed Division of the USSS: "He has an excellent reputation. He's won way more than he's lost with the Secret Service. I've heard he's a ballbuster and won't back down when they play their intimidation games." Shortly after SAIC Domingo told me that the service wouldn't be continuing my employment, I made an appointment and went to see Peter, though I still had about two weeks left at WFO. Sitting still and letting the time run out was not an option. There were deadlines looming for me to consider—appeals, EEO complaints, grievance procedures—and who knew what else they might want me to miss out on due to their strict limitations.

Peter's office was on the eleventh floor of a building on K Street, a posh part of town I'd often found myself in on protection assignments, escorting dignitaries. As a rookie, I was usually posted on the street; I rarely made it past the doors of the embassies and office buildings. Now, a receptionist was directing me to a dark wood-covered waiting room filled with paintings and a fancy rug.

"Mr. Carre will be with you shortly, Ms. Wilkas," she said from the doorway.

"Thank you," I said and smiled at her before she breezed back down the long hallway. She might have been twenty-five—not much younger than me—but the skirt she wore didn't look very practical. Was it elegant? It definitely fit the surroundings better than my black slacks and jacket. I straightened my clothes as I sat on the leather couch, and I reached over to pick up a magazine from the glass-topped coffee table. The room wasn't big, but it was nice, classy. As I leafed through the

Economist, I wondered how a place could be so comfortable and still fill me with such a sense of dread. And then the questions started to pop into my head, one by one. How much was this going to cost? How long would this drag on for? What if I didn't like him? What would he ask me? I still wasn't comfortable talking about the details of what had happened, mostly because I was still sorting it out myself. Also it was pretty emotional for me, and I wanted to ride that roller coaster alone.

Finally, Peter came into the room. He was about forty and well dressed. He looked like he would have been at home at a conference table with the bankers and statesmen in the magazine I was reading. But maybe that meeting would be taking place in the tropics, because he was tan—very tan for May in DC. I'd later learn that it was a perpetual state for him, a little bit of vanity that went right along with his friendly and slightly arrogant demeanor. I liked him from the get-go. He was easy to talk to, and he carried himself like he knew he was a capable, intelligent counselor. It gave me faith that he knew what he was doing taking on an agency of the US government, even as his expensive suit made me wonder if I'd be able to afford to hire him.

"Mary Beth. It's nice to meet you. Let's go sit down in my office." I got up when he came over to shake my hand, and together we walked down the hall and into his office. Peter turned to me and said, "First of all, I'm sorry that you're going through all of this. Why don't you walk me through everything that's happened?"

Over the course of several hour-long meetings in the next weeks, Peter and I went over everything that had happened with the USSS and in my FBI applications, with me adding more and more detail each time we met. As we wrapped up one of those sessions, he laid out our next steps.

"I'm going to request your personnel file. I want to see what they said about you in training. I want to see whether there's anything about your time in WFO. Essentially, I want to see if there's anything in your file that will help or hurt us," he said.

I don't know if it was the idea that I was being put under scrutiny again—by my own lawyer—or the whopper of a first invoice I had just received from him, but my concern must have shown on my face. Peter noticed.

He said, "Mary Beth, you're paying me to do a job. Part of that job is to do the worrying on this case. So you don't need to worry too. That's what you're paying me to do." Fair enough, I thought. It was a huge shift in mindset, but surprisingly, I actually did feel some relief. And, as I found with time, I hardly ever thought about the case, unless there was a meeting, a deadline, or a document to sign.

Peter talked me through the grievance process, and on May 29, 1992, one day before my contract with the Service was set to expire, I submitted an Administrative Grievance Form contesting the expiration of term appointment. On the form, I stated, "Grievant wants the termination notice to be rescinded." Then, under the section headed "To clarify grievance issues," I wrote, "Grievant submits that the adverse personnel action has been taken on the basis of mistaken information and interpretation of language on employment applications. Grievant has also been denied due process of law. Grievant has also been subject to disparate treatment."

In June, I consulted with a USSS Equal Employment Opportunity (EEO) counselor just to cover all my bases and hear what they might have to say. After having been urged to several times, I also contacted the head of the USSS Women Agents Association. In these conversations, I was either informed how to pursue and/or was blatantly encouraged to pursue a path that I was not interested in—because it would have meant claiming something that was absolutely not true. It would have meant dropping that ugly term that makes government agencies and corporations alike recoil: *sexual discrimination*. I did not feel that I had been treated unjustly nor was I currently being treated adversely because I was a woman. I was starting to get angry that, for almost everyone I talked to, gender discrimination seemed to be the automatic, go-to claim. It's one thing to ask whether I had experienced any disparate treatment that I would attribute to me being a female. It's another thing to outright push this tactic and make major assumptions without asking the appropriate questions.

By mid-July, Peter and I had begun to create a strategy for our case to the USSS, running through different approaches in his office on K Street. He'd scribbled some notes on a pad, but his handwriting made them impossible to read. Still, I was pretty sure I knew where he was going.

"I have some ideas, Mary Beth, but ultimately, the decision is yours. Sexual harassment?"

"In the little over a year that I worked as a USSS Agent, I was never sexually harassed."

Peter raised his hands, his palms facing me from across the desk, and lowered his head just a bit. He looked at me with his steely blue eyes.

"Do you feel like you were a victim of sexual discrimination as an agent with the USSS?"

"No, Peter," I groaned.

"Not even by IA?"

Another groan. "The IA inspectors were assholes. They immediately assumed my guilt. They were dead wrong. They weren't looking for the truth, they were on a witch hunt. They were abusing their power."

"So did—"

"No. Again, they were assholes, but I think they would have been assholes if I were male, too."

I understood that as my lawyer, he had to cover his bases, but this was really getting tired. I had a feeling I knew what was coming next.

Before he could get to it, there was a knock on his office door. His receptionist was wearing red today and carrying a tray with two cups of coffee on it, along with sugar and pink Sweet'N Low packets. After she left, Peter continued.

"I've been looking into the other cases, Mary Beth."

I grabbed the mug of coffee nearest me. Peter knew that I had three excellent sources now, in addition to ASAIC Tommy Castile from the Washington Field Office, who had pointed me to the cases of six male USSS Special Agents and even a major incident involving one of the IA inspectors on my case. All of those agents were still on the job with the USSS, yet they had all allegedly committed a variety of illegal offenses or had legal run-ins that would have knocked them out of the running to be USSS Agents and/or should have gotten them kicked out of the Service—DUI, DUI and assault, cocaine use, cocaine purchase, robbery, and a bizarre botched diamond recovery operation (as in, the diamonds were now missing). My favorite story was of three agents at the largest USSS field office who were involved in cocaine issues—one for buying and two for using, and not one of them suffered any repercussions. Two of those six individuals whose cases were brought to my attention had allegedly failed polygraph examinations on their specific allegations and were still on the job. Of course, it didn't hurt that one of them was allegedly the son of a former speaker of the house. Some of the alleged misdeeds had taken place prior to these agents being hired and others while they were serving as USSS Agents. According to my sources, the USSS knew about every one of these agents' transgressions, yet they chose to keep the information under wraps and either hire them or keep them on the job.

Peter's investigation had so far led him to confirm that four of these allegations were true. He was still in the process of confirming the other two. I didn't ask who his sources were, but I was impressed that Peter had been able to substantiate the juicy incriminating information on four of the agents already.

"We have a case here, Mary Beth."

I had been thinking about this. A lot. I took a sip of coffee before answering.

"Peter." I paused a couple of seconds, looking right at Peter's steely blue eyes, and exhaled. "Even if every single one of those cases is true, what does what those other agents have done have to do with me?"

"It shows that the USSS looks the other way when it suits them. Plus, they were all male."

If I used this strategy and won, I knew I would always be one of "those" agents. One of the ones that got into hot water with the Service, was let go, and was brought back because I sued based on bullshit precedent and/or sexual discrimination—not based on their poor judgment, their mishandling of the IA investigation, or their decision to appease the FBI. I would be an agent everyone whispered about. I would be an agent people, especially supervisors, treated with kid gloves for fear I was sue happy. I would be one of those agents that male agents did not interact with so as not to get wrapped up in a dreaded sexual discrimination case. Fuck that. I wasn't going to blackmail the Service into letting me back in.

"I don't want the USSS to look the other way. I want them to do what's right!"

"The fact that they haven't in this case shows that their treatment of you is disparate, Mary Beth. We know they'd do it for a male agent and we have four, soon to be six, cases that prove that."

Black coffee splashed onto the tray and onto the pink packets of artificial sweetener as I set my mug down.

"No." I was practically yelling at Peter now. I ran my fingers through my hair and stood up from my chair. I faced him and took a deep breath. "For the last time, Peter," I said, holding up my right hand, using fingers one by one to make my next points, "I'm not going to claim sexual harassment. I'm not going to allege I was treated differently because I was a woman. I'm not going to align myself with the irrelevant bullshit of other agents. I don't care about them. I want to fight my own fight. A clean one. One that is 100 percent about me. My case, my situation, my circumstances." I sat back down and just looked at Peter, maybe even challenging him a little with my look.

Peter reached for a napkin and wiped up the coffee on the tray. I thought he'd be surprised by my decision, but he slowly smiled. Maybe he already knew what my answer would be, I don't know.

"OK, Mary Beth. That makes my job a hell of a lot easier. No tangential issues, no more digging around for evidence, no bullshit."

That was a huge relief to me. I was the one that had to look myself in the mirror after this was all over. What the Service had done to me was unfair—complete bullshit, actually—and I'd fight it, but I wouldn't lie about it. That was a fishing expedition I was not interested in. Plus, as far as I was concerned, footing the bill for continued exploration into corrupt agents was a waste of money and one that would have zero return on investment for me and my case.

The next morning, my roommate Nancy knocked on my bedroom door and woke me. When I turned to the clock, I saw that it was 10:00 a.m.

"God, Nancy. I feel like I'm sleeping so much these days."

"That's because you're depressed, Mary Beth."

What? Was she right?

She continued. "Look, I know it's hard, but you've got to keep living your life."

It's not like I wasn't living my life. I was meeting with Peter and strategizing at least once a week. And besides, why not wake up late? It's not like I had a job to get to. I took care of my business. Just this past week, I'd gotten some overdue dry cleaning done, called the phone company and cleared up a weird charge on my bill, rented some movies. I'd gone on an interview with a well-known investigative firm. Called a couple of friends. Gotten Chinese food. Gone to the movies . . .

I looked up at Nancy from my bed, bright sunlight from the window hitting her. I tossed off the blanket.

"I'm going for a run. Thanks, Nancy."

I had a lot on my mind that morning. For one, I was thinking about how the government had their own lawyers, unlimited funds, and all the time in the world. If my case wasn't resolved soon, I didn't know what I'd do. How long could I really hold out? And, what was my plan B?

So, on that run down to Arlington, I thought about, for the first time, all that I'd still have, even if the USSS case didn't go my way: my reputation, for one. As long as I didn't say or base my case on anything that was untrue, I would still be known as a solid agent. One who'd had some kind of an application snafu maybe, but a good and solid agent. I'd still have my integrity and the ability to hold my head up. I'd be able to face my parents and not cringe at the thought that I'd lied and violated what they'd taught me about right and wrong. That is what mattered to me most. As I ran on, I realized that, while I'd take this fight as far as I could, there were things much more important to me than the United States Secret Service.

This was one of my most pivotal realizations. Yes, the Secret Service meant a lot to me. But being a USSS Agent was not who I was; it was what I did for a living. If things did not work out, I would still be the same person, just one that had experienced a major redirection that sent me down a totally unforeseen fork in the road.

At my next meeting with Peter, I was impressed—but not surprised—at how meticulous he'd been. He'd combed through all the information: every document I had given him, every document the USSS had provided him, and every case he could get his hands on that had been brought against the USSS that might help my case. Together we put together an offensive we felt was winnable and that we could both stand behind.

The next few months were filled with letters and phone calls between my attorney and the attorney for the USSS, Natalie Persons, regarding my official grievance and appeal for the USSS to modify their decision to release me from employment as a Special Agent. Fortunately, in the interim, I had landed a contract to do a high-threat protection assignment, and it was taking me overseas—to Peru with the Organization of American States (OAS). Being out of Washington, DC, was just what I needed to clear my head and focus on something other than my case. Unbeknownst to me at the time, it would also be an invaluable entry on my resume.

I was in my hotel room in Lima when I got a message that Peter had called. We hadn't scheduled an appointment to talk, so I knew there must be some news on his end. As I sat on the bed and called him back from the phone on my nightstand in my tiny room, I hoped he had good news for me.

"Okay, this is what they're offering us, Mary Beth," Peter said, after the receptionist put me through. He went on to describe the USSS's offer of a settlement agreement. He read to me from a draft of the document: "In consideration for the opportunity to make an oral presentation and written supplement before and to the Director, Ms. Wilkas agrees that by her signature on this Settlement Agreement and Release, she waives, releases, and forever forswears any EEO claim or charge, or any other claim or charge, which she may or may not have against the Secret Service, the Department of the Treasury, any current or former employee of the Secret Service, and/or any current or former employee of the Department of the Treasury."

They were giving me what I wanted—a chance to make my case, to appeal to the person at the Service that made the decisions, the director.

"This is our only option, isn't it?" I asked.

"I think it's a good offer, Mary Beth."

I understood the position of the USSS; they had experienced and continued to experience a tremendous number of legal claims for a broad range of issues, and they wanted this legal brouhaha over and done with. Peter and I discussed the pros and cons of signing this agreement, and, in the end, we both felt this was the best we were going to do—be granted an "audience" with the director of the Service. Even if it meant putting all of our eggs in one basket and allowing the government the upper hand in the end, I had to sign.

Peter had his receptionist fax the agreement over to my hotel. I signed it and faxed it back. I was headed back to the States at the end of the month for my brother's wedding, so we scheduled the meeting with the director then.

I looked out my window—it wasn't a bad view, if you disregarded the tanks and soldiers on the street. I took a deep breath. No matter how things went, at least I knew now that this nightmare would be over soon. I'd get my say. Not under the hot lights of IA but, rather, in front of someone I hoped would be objective, sensible, and fair.

On October 29, 1992, I followed Peter into a Washington, DC, conference room in USSS headquarters. It all felt so surreal. I almost couldn't believe it was actually happening. The day had finally arrived—my chance to have my say, to make my appeal for my job directly to the director of the USSS, Peter Mick. This was my opportunity to clear up the misjudgments and clear my name. My adrenaline was flowing—no, it was completely flooding my body.

I'd never met Director Mick before that day, since I'd graduated training under the previous director only about a year and a half earlier. I knew Mick had become a Special Agent twenty-five years before and that he was known around WFO as being a stern, but decent, person. As a young agent, I would normally have been intimidated but proud to meet the director of the Service, but these circumstances were different. Now, I had to do more than make a good impression. I was facing the man who would decide my professional fate.

I looked at the other people gathered in the room. A petite blonde attorney from the Service's Office of Chief Counsel adjusted the bow tie on her power suit and checked her watch. A personnel officer from the Service smiled at me, and the stenographer sat at the ready. The director sat stock-still. His affect was completely flat. My only chance was to get through to him, without any of the red-tape bullshit, one agent to another.

I stole a glance at Peter who, in his three-piece suit and tan, was calmly unpacking paperwork from his leather briefcase.

"Why don't we get started?" It was the attorney. She continued, "Director Mick?"

"By my watch, it's 3:34 p.m. on Thursday, October 29, 1992." The director went on, introducing the people in the room, stating the purpose of the meeting. His words seemed to be for the benefit of the stenographer more than anyone else in the room. He continued, "This is your opportunity, Mary, to present whatever information you wish me to consider in this matter."

"Thank you," Peter answered almost immediately. He pushed his hair back and shot the cuffs of his suit forward before going on. "I think you should know, if you don't already, that Mary Elizabeth Wilkas is a very talented, hardworking, bilingual, valuable Special Agent of the Secret Service." No one in the room seemed particularly impressed by Peter's bold opening statement.

"Among her qualities, as those who will have worked with her can certainly vouch for, is honesty, honesty in the extreme if that can be said." Peter's voice had begun to boom as he puffed himself up in his chair. He lifted his hand, pointed his index finger, and paused, ensuring that he had the attention of everyone in the room, especially the director.

"She's very detail-oriented, sort of hair-splitting almost." For the first time, the director's eyebrow lifted as he watched Peter's finger dive with a thud onto the conference table. As his arm bounced back onto the armrest of his chair, I had to contain a flinch to avoid being hit. "Working as her attorney, I've come to discover that. I think that has been reflected in the approach she has taken to her job—she always utilizes a correct and precise manner toward every task she is given." I was starting to feel like I was listening to my own—or maybe my USSS career's—eulogy.

"I believe we will find that this is reflected in the very documents that she has filled out for application for employment with the Secret Service, which have been what, after all, has caused some of this controversy and caused the expiration of her appointment. Yet, when we examine this, I think you will see the reason why the approach she took was the honest and correct one and will demonstrate her integrity, rather than a lack thereof."

He laid out—again—everything in the case: the shoplifting incident, the hash use, my application to the FBI, the IA investigation. The director remained impassive. The personnel officer looked bored. The government lawyer was staring at Peter. I was mesmerized—I had no idea what Peter had prepared for this meeting. He wasn't done.

"Now, I know that my client loves this work. She's really good at it. She has integrity. She's fearless. Being a Special Agent with the United States Secret Service was a dream come true for her. She's agreed to terms in this settlement agreement, against much advice, I must admit, that basically deprived her of all her rights. She doesn't want back pay. She doesn't want legal fees. She doesn't want any damages. She doesn't even want a right to appeal your decision. That shows how confident she is that she is right. That she has been honest, that there has been a mix-up made by those investigating her, that there has been a poor decision made to allow her appointment to expire. But I believe it's important that she tell you a little bit about her reasons for wanting to come back to this job. Mary Beth should also speak about how she feels."

What? My head snapped to Peter. He hadn't told me to expect this or to prepare anything. I thought he would be the only one speaking today, since he was there representing me. Peter just smiled back at me. It was the first moment of silence in the room for a long while. Shit.

At last, the director spoke. "All right."

All eyes were on me.

"Do you have any questions?" It was all I could muster on the spot, trying to buy time so I could think of what I was going to say.

"Not right now," the director answered.

"OK . . . Peter's right. I have, in the settlement agreement, given up a lot." Whatever I was going to say, I figured, now was my chance to just say it. I looked the director right in the eyes. I wasn't talking to anyone else in the room.

"I just want my job back. The Secret Service to me represents what I've worked for the better part of my life. It's how I chose my university. It's how I chose, you know, the life I've led since then, really the life I've led all my life. It's what I'm very good at. It's what I enjoy. It's what's been very good to me. It's been very gratifying.

"And the day I stepped—when I was let go, I got so much support from people. It really reassured me. It made me realize that all my hard work was not overlooked. It was really valued. It wasn't for nothing. All the hard work, all those years of educating myself, of working for what I worked for.

"I've learned a lot from this whole situation. I've learned the value of this job, you know, having it taken away from me, realizing how much—how good I was at it and how good it was to me."

Peter had explained to them what had gone wrong. I'd told the director what the job meant to me. If he didn't understand that, there was nothing left to say.

The USSS lawyer bent over in her chair to the director and whispered in his ear. They asked for a moment to step outside of the room to confer. Peter and I—and the stenographer and personnel officer—just sat in silence.

When they came back into the room, the director asked me some questions about my past for a few minutes before the lawyer took over.

"Maybe if I could take this just a step further. I think one of the concerns that the Secret Service had was that you applied to the FBI and were subsequently rejected. And then it appears that what you put on the SF 86 and SF 86A for the USSS is different than what you put on the FBI application, the idea being that maybe you consciously thought about it and decided not to tell the truth. Do you think you could respond to that?"

It was the IA line of questioning all over again. I responded. "That's not true. Knowing the way—how scrupulous—the process of being hired for any federal agency is, to think that I'm going to hide something . . . anything would be discovered. And there's the polygraph. All of these forms that have to be filled out. You have to swear to everything you say and everything you fill out. If I didn't believe all of that to be true, I don't think I could sit here today. I mean . . ." I had to pause for a moment, to swallow my anger—or was it disappointment? "I'm sorry, but I don't live my life like that."

Not an hour after we began, Director Mick thanked me, looked over to the USSS lawyer, and said he had no other questions. The lawyer looked at Peter and me and stated that the meeting had concluded. They would notify us of their decision as soon as it was made.

I had a flight to Chicago soon after. The rehearsal dinner for my brother's wedding fell on Halloween. I was staying at the house of one of my sisters, as were my parents. I broached the topic of the meeting with the director with my mother. My father was downtown for a quarterly meeting for a board he'd sat on since they'd left Chicago.

"Mom, I have something to tell you."

I thought back to the conference room in DC, the director and lawyers all talking about me, my future. I was terrified at the time, but I wasn't going to let anybody there see it. *Never let them see you sweat.* I had learned it from my mother: as a nurse, as a parent, she had always been completely unflappable. Of course, I knew she loved me, but she didn't show emotion easily. That's why I was shocked when I saw dread on her face at my announcement.

"Oh God, are you pregnant?"

I laughed. To my staunch Catholic mother, me being pregnant and unmarried was about the worst news she could imagine. When I told her what had happened in DC, it didn't seem quite as bad anymore, to either of us. She was, as she always had been, extremely supportive and encouraging. My father was as well, when my mother and I sat down with him that evening.

After the wedding, I flew back to Lima, Peru, where I was still working the protection gig with OAS while waiting to hear the final verdict from the Service. Somewhere in the back of my mind, I thought I might have gotten through to the director. It was more than a month later, in December, when Peter called with news. This time, he happened to catch me in my hotel room.

He read to me from the letter he had received from the USSS, the director's final decision regarding my case: "It is my determination that you intentionally provided false information on security clearance forms, and the decision of Assistant Director Shafter to release you from employment with the Secret Service was proper."

I was not going back to work as a Special Agent for the USSS. I was literally speechless.

Eventually, Peter started talking just to fill the dead air. "Mary Beth, you have a bright career ahead of you. Do not let this—"

"God, Peter, I just thought it was going to . . . I really thought it was going to go our way."

"I'm sorry, Mary Beth."

The hotel in Lima was close to the beach, where I would go for long runs, like the one I eventually took after some long quiet moments once I hung up with Peter. To get to the water, I had to walk past the two tanks stationed outside the hotel for security. As I ran along the sea, I had to tighten the strap of my fanny pack so that the pistol I carried in it didn't bounce uncomfortably. It still jostled a bit with every step—not a problem I'd had in DC, in Spain, or in Chicago, but one of many changes I'd have to get used to as I ran, lived, and worked from here on out.

CHAPTER 5

LIMA, PERU
1992

"And you must be the ambassador's secretary?" I was asked for what felt like the hundredth time.

And, for what felt like the hundredth time, I smiled and said, "Of course." *How many secretaries*, I wondered, *carry 9mm handguns?*

In another meeting, an aide, squinting his eyes and stepping a bit too close for comfort, said, "Ah, you must be the ambassador's daughter!"

"Si, claro," I answered. After all, who couldn't see the family resemblance between the short, rotund Colombian ambassador and me, a tall, athletic Lithuanian by way of Chicago?

Secretary, daughter, oh, and my personal favorite—mistress. Rumors about who I was and what exactly I was doing hanging around the ambassador made their way around Lima at lightning speed. Even though I didn't find the speculation to be very amusing, the ambassador, truth be told, really got a kick out of it.

In the lobby of the Hotel Las Americas the day I arrived, the general manager grinned and nodded at me, almost leering. I'd just requested for my room to be moved next to the ambassador's.

"*Security reasons?* I'm sorry, señorita. I am not sure I understand your request. My English isn't very good."

He'd understood me just fine. I had been speaking Spanish, after all.

I was in Peru on my first private protection assignment, a position I'd taken while I worked my way through my USSS appeal. My job was to protect the ambassador of an election observation mission for OAS, and to do my job, I needed to have the hotel room flanking the ambassador's. My partner had already been given the room to the left of the ambassador's, but I'd been assigned one a few doors away. My first order of business was to get our sleeping quarters squared away and secure, with an agent on either side of the VIP.

Of course, I couldn't mention that the ambassador was, in fact, my protectee or that my colleague and I were security agents. Sure, he knew who the OAS ambassador was, but as far as the hotel manager was concerned, the rest of us were election observers working for the organization.

I let the manager smirk and think what he wanted. As long as he didn't get in the way of me getting my job done, I didn't care if he mistook me for Elvis. Anyway, it wouldn't be long before he figured out that I was part of the protection team. The ambassador had a busy schedule, and surely seeing a woman leading the way to these appointments would strike the manager as more than a little unusual for a high-class escort. So, for now, I just rolled my eyes and repeated myself for the third time as the smirk on his face widened. *Well, you're not in Kansas anymore, Wilkas*, I thought. I was getting a taste of protection work without having the USSS, the badge, and all the prestige and privilege it afforded in my corner. So far it was a little sweet, a little sour.

The Organization of American States, the entity that had brought me to Peru, was founded in 1948 as a kind of League of Nations of the Americas, and it is dedicated to working for peace and strengthening democracy in North and South America. One of the ways it does that is by providing election monitoring. The OAS has an excellent reputation for what it calls "independent, impartial observation of elections" to ensure that they are "free, peaceful and transparent," but making sure that was the case in Peru in 1992 would be tricky.

In April of that year, Alberto Fujimori, Peru's president, had suspended the nation's constitution, dissolved Congress, and purged the judiciary. Fujimori's drastic action was, he insisted to the public, a reaction to the leftist guerrilla group known as the Sendero Luminoso (Shining Path), which had been engaged in a campaign of insurgency, assassinations, and bombings in Peru since 1980. These Maoist guerrillas were fervently opposed to what they called intervention by "Yankee imperialists," and Fujimori, with the widespread support of the Peruvian people, was frustrated by what he viewed as congressional obstruction in combatting them.

In the aftermath of Fujimori's so-called "auto-coup," the government of Peru had formally invited the secretary general of the OAS to send observers to "verify the transparency" of the new congressional and municipal elections in Peru, which were to take place in November 1992 and January 1993, respectively. The OAS was a peaceful and impartial organization, but now it would be responsible for a group of more than two hundred international observers in a violent, unstable nation where its representatives would be targeted by guerillas. Groups like the Sendero Luminoso didn't exactly welcome the OAS with open arms. Although the organization was international, it was based in Washington, DC, and as such, it was viewed as a "Yankee" institution. For the first time in its history, the organization was forced to contemplate hiring security agents to protect their ambassador and the members of its election monitoring mission. They ultimately decided that doing this mission without security would be too much of a liability. I was one of the eight members chosen for that security team.

Besides the fact that Lima was far more dangerous than even the iffy parts of DC I had been conducting investigations in, the protection detail for the OAS would be nothing like my work in the Secret Service. For one, the team was much smaller. The USSS is a massive law enforcement agency with the resources of the federal government behind it. After all, the USSS is responsible for protecting the leader of the free world, the president of the United States. Thus, the USSS does not typically skimp on the number of protective agents sent to any site, for any planned or unplanned event, or even for "routine" stops. The OAS, on the other hand, had only been able to budget for eight security agents, and it seemed like even that might have been a stretch.

But the small size of the security team in Peru was not just a matter of resources. The primary protectee and chief of the electoral observation mission, the OAS ambassador, had already completed an advance trip of sorts to Peru to discuss the mission with Peruvian government officials. During this visit, he was offered all the bells and whistles that went along with a high-profile, high-threat dignitary in Peru—three main motorcade vehicles, police lead and tail cars, motorcycles, an ambulance, and nearly an army of Peruvian police protection agents. However, the ambassador had his own ideas. He politely refused the top-tier security package on the grounds that this approach would be more of a magnet for attacks than it would be functional protection. And the OAS ambassador, unlike someone under the protection of the Secret Service, had the final say in his protection plan. He agreed to a two-car motorcade with two Peruvian police drivers, and that was it.

From an outsider's perspective, this might not seem like a prudent decision. However, understand that a high-threat, high-profile protectee does not necessarily call for a high-profile protection package and a high-profile motorcade. Conversely, a low-profile, low-threat protectee does not necessarily equate to a low-profile protection package and a low-profile motorcade. I have been in 100-car motorcades in Washington, DC, for dignitaries that no one would have had a clue as to who they were, and I have been in two-car motorcades where the person I was protecting was very well known and a likely target of terrorism. The ambassador had it right: excessive, attention-grabbing security packages can draw attention and paint a target on a protectee's back.

I was up for the job in Lima because, besides working for the USSS, I had worked for the Center for Democracy. I was considered a Latin America expert, and I had already coordinated and co-managed election observation missions in El Salvador and Guatemala (though not on the security side). My experience in the USSS, my Spanish-language skills, my travel experience, and my knowledge of how election observation missions worked made me an excellent candidate.

Still, I was a bit nervous when it was time for my final interview with the ambassador. I had had no problem convincing the other people I interviewed with that I was capable, willing, and ready for this mission, but I had no idea whether the ambassador would want a female on his protection team. I was pleasantly surprised when the ambassador stood at the end of the interview and said to all those present, "There is nothing like the protection of a woman. Hire her." At first, I didn't know what to make of those words, but my smile grew when I understood what he meant. It was a shrewd bit of strategy on the ambassador's part; what he realized was that, in a country as chauvinistic as Peru was at the time, I was the last person anyone would think was part of his security team.

I was thrilled to get the position. Seeing as I was still locked in a fight to keep my job with the Secret Service, I felt tremendously fortunate that my attorney had referred me to the Investigative Group, Inc. (IGI) in Washington, DC, in June 1992. IGI was a well-known investigative firm founded by Terry Lenzner, a former Watergate prosecutor. I was the youngest investigator they had ever considered hiring, so they decided to do a "look see" to make sure I would fit in, hiring me on a contract vs. a full-time basis. To be honest, more than I needed the work, I needed this sign that— even with everything that was happening—I would still have a future in this profession on both the protection and investigative sides. After working at IGI for a couple of months, I knew that the OAS gig was a solid possibility. Hence, I let my supervisor at IGI know about the OAS job. Not only was he gracious in assuring me I would still have a job at IGI when I returned from Lima, he thought the opportunity was a very cool one.

As ready as I was to get to work in Peru, delay after delay kept us in the United States. I watched the news, and with each new development, I became more worried that the OAS mission would be permanently scratched. Then, news came that the Peruvian government had arrested the leader of the Sendero Luminoso, Abimael Guzman, the nation's most wanted man for over a decade, along with several other guerillas. While this was a huge success for Peru, no one knew what the aftermath of the arrest might bring. Regardless, the decision was made to launch the OAS mission.

Two weeks before departing for Lima, I learned more about the current security situation on the ground in Peru in a briefing at the OAS offices. *Yikes.* The USSS briefing rooms could be pretty drab, but this was downright shabby. Along with the security company's managers, the whole field team was assembled in a DC office—eight of us intently focused on what our mission was going to look like, at least at this point. Four of us would be based in Lima, while the other four would be sent out to more remote areas of Peru where OAS offices were being set up for the election observation mission. Twenty to thirty international observers from the OAS election observation group would be working in each of those offices. I did not envy my four teammates being sent to the more remote parts of the country. Tight budget or not, no one in my role ever wanted to be the single person on site responsible for the safety of a group.

I was ready to analyze, scrutinize, and play out potential scenarios and logistical challenges of the mission, like we would have done in WFO, but the briefing was scant on operational details. It devolved instead into a discussion of administrative minutiae: availability, pay scale, vacation days, hotel bookings. I took the opportunity to measure up the other people—all men—I'd be working with. For the most part, they were on the older end for protection agents, and, though I didn't know any of their backgrounds, their appearances did not instill confidence in me. They were dressed in khaki pants and polo shirts, and most of them were short and not in good shape. The guy running the mission mentioned that he was Cuban American, and immediately I pictured the whole crew in Miami. No, no, we're not talking Crockett and Tubbs from *Miami Vice*—I mean the old guys playing cards down by the beach they'd pump for information. They didn't have the bearing of protection agents at all, and the whole scene struck me as unprofessional. This wasn't a question of being judgmental—I *like* playing cards on the beach in Miami!—but what we'd be doing was serious and, oh, dangerous work. It was only smart that I understood what I was getting into and with whom.

Thankfully, there was one exception to this seeming group of Keystone Cops. The partner I'd been assigned, Mike, was rugged, tough looking, and hardly ever smiled. Mike had a Special Forces background and, thankfully, a few contacts in Lima to assist us with information. We got along great, for which I was most thankful. I instantly respected him and considered him a big brother figure, though he gave me more shit than any of my siblings ever did. He quickly gave me the nickname "Agent 99." He was Hawaiian, so I, in turn, called him "5-0." Both names stuck.

Lima, Peru, 1992, "Agent 99" and "5-0"

On February 11, 1992, approximately eight months before we arrived in country, a Sendero Luminoso car bomb loaded with almost ninety pounds of dynamite exploded outside the US ambassador's residence in Lima, killing three Peruvian policemen and causing extensive damage to the structure. Fortunately, neither the ambassador nor his wife were in the residence at the time of the explosion. Minutes prior to the primary attack, two smaller, diversionary explosions were set off nearby, distracting embassy guards and policemen. The bombing was bold and well-orchestrated.

The "Tarata bombing" was even more brazen and successful and put fear into both the local and the international communities. In fact, it was the deadliest Sendero Luminoso bombing in the history of their long conflict in Peru. On July 16, 1992, two trucks, each packed with 12,205 pounds of explosives, were detonated on Tarata Street in the upscale neighborhood of Miraflores in Lima. The damage was devastating: 25 people were killed, 155 more were wounded, and the explosions destroyed or damaged 63 parked vehicles, 183 homes, and 400 businesses. This attack symbolized the inception of a week-long assault against the Peruvian government that caused forty deaths and eventually shut down most of the capital.

We arrived in Lima less than three months after the Tarata bombing and settled in just blocks away from where it had taken place in the Miraflores neighborhood, in the beautiful Hotel Las Americas. Near Lima's beaches, shops, and financial center, the hotel had not been damaged in the July blasts, but you could not help but be put off by the two tanks parked in the doorway of the hotel, along with the cadre of heavily armed military men in uniform in and around the hotel. It was clear that the government of Peru took the threats of the Sendero Luminoso seriously, and they were going to do their best to prevent an international incident. In fact, we would learn that they were doing more than we expected—or had asked.

The OAS ambassador was the point man on the election observation. Due to the nature of his mission, the ambassador had plans to travel all over Lima and the country to determine whether the entire election process was, in fact, "free and fair." He'd get around the country via the more developed airports and roads located in and around the capital. The situation in Peru was tense, but the ambassador had made it clear that he intended to bring only me and my colleague for protection when he traveled. An army of Peruvian police agents would only cause trouble, he determined.

The hotel was buzzing. More than two hundred of our election observers from over a dozen countries, a large team of OAS staff from Washington, DC, the OAS ambassador, and our security team had arrived. After a few days in Lima, about half of the observers, staff, and security agents headed out to their respective locations across Peru. As our team got settled into a routine, we began to get familiar with the hotel staff and the police. One afternoon after returning from a meeting, Mike turned to me after we'd gotten the ambassador tucked away in his room.

"Agent 99, come outside with me for a second," he said. We exited the lobby and chatted with the guards standing duty by the tanks. Before we went back inside, Mike tapped my shoulder and leaned in to whisper to me.

"There's a guy on the corner, smoking. Second time today."

I turned back to the guards in the tank, saying, "Hasta luego. Gracias!" As I smiled and waved, I looked over the tank's nose and took a mental picture of the guy in a long-sleeved shirt, smoking alone and leaning on a trash can.

The next day, when Mike headed out with the ambassador, I stayed back for a bit. The same guy was on the corner, leaning on the trash can and letting his cigarette burn down as he followed our protectee with his eyes. Then, the morning after, while the ambassador slept, Mike and I headed down to the lobby. In the quiet of the morning, we could spot the smoker through the window of the hotel's front door.

"OK, we've seen this guy too many times," Mike said.

"For sure. It doesn't look like he has a weapon on him, at least," I replied.

In the USSS, I would have had to radio the suspicious individual in, and someone else would have determined if there was a threat while Mike and I ensured that the protectee was secure. Now, I knew that even if we called the security managers that were with us, they didn't have anybody else to call in. And they certainly would not volunteer to handle this situation.

"Management won't do shit." Mike had come to the same conclusion in his own way. He looked me square in the eye. "Keep an eye on me, 99. I'm going to go talk to him."

There wasn't much else to do and nothing to say. I took up a good position and watched as Mike approached the guy. After a minute of friendly conversation, the man smiled broadly and pulled his shirt up for Mike. There was no weapon, just the glint of a badge. When we met with our police liaison later that day, they confirmed what the smoker had told Mike: he was an undercover cop there to monitor the area and assist us. Another layer of protection, courtesy of the Peruvian government.

Assassinating political candidates and setting off bombs had become the modus operandi for the Sendero Luminoso guerrillas, especially after Guzman's arrest. During our five-month mission in Peru, the Sendero Luminoso car-bombed two Coca-Cola plants, truck-bombed the Lima headquarters of IBM, and fired at an American Airlines jet as it taxied into Lima's airport. Bomb threats at our OAS offices were a weekly occurrence, (consistent) electricity was a luxury, and it was common for the city to virtually shut down due to the fear the Sendero Luminoso had put into working-class people. Oh yeah, and during the first week of our stay in Lima, a bomb went off in a building in our neighborhood, about three blocks away. It was a building that was next to the hotel where many Canadian election observers were staying (they were part of a different election observation mission), and, per the report Mike and I received from the Peruvian police, most of those observers left the next day. This created a bit of a shitstorm of worry among our observers, but in the end, they all opted to remain in country.

We were grateful for the cooperation of the Peruvian national police when we got it, but we came to realize it wasn't guaranteed.

"What's going on?" I asked the two security company managers sitting across the table from me. I had been called in to a meeting to discuss my write-up of an incident. Even two days later, in a conference room in our hotel, the incident still felt unreal, almost like a scene from a movie.

I had been corralling the ambassador along with a group of OAS election observers who, by proxy, were also my protectees that evening. I was trying to get them back home safely after a late night of partying. As the group started getting into our van, a male, about 40 years old, walked or, rather, stumbled from across the street, bottle of booze in hand, and lurched toward the ambassador, who was laughing with one of the younger observers. I immediately stepped in front of the ambassador and, over my shoulder, told him to get in the van. He didn't listen to me, however. He'd had a few drinks and seemed to be feeling a little feisty. The other man was also clearly inebriated. He had long, stringy hair, an unshaven face, and dark, bloodshot eyes. He reminded me of a drunk pirate. About twenty feet behind him, his similarly grungy-looking friends watched.

The pirate began yelling at the ambassador over my shoulder. I insisted to the ambassador that he get in the van, but some of the van's passengers, other observers, had gotten curious at the ruckus and were trying to make their way back out of the van to spectate.

Keeping my eye on the drunk guy, I was adamant with them: sit your asses down in the van, and shut up. But I was polite, at least sort of. They started to follow instructions, but . . .

"Who the fuck do you think you are, lady?" the man snapped at me. I already had an extendable baton out, unbeknownst to anyone.

But, now, I was rehearsing in my head the dropping of my baton and pulling out of my weapon.

"Inside. Back in the van. Now." I was talking to the ambassador, but I didn't take my eyes off of the man.

"I'm talking to your boss, not you, *puta*!" Okay, he just called me a whore.

At last, the ambassador realized this was not a joke, wised up, and stepped into the van.

"Hey!" The man threw his bottle into the street beside me, shattering the glass. Suddenly, he was in my face. He smelled like shit—his breath, his clothes, his bright-red face. I gave him a push, and he stumbled backward. He was spitting as he hurled every curse he could call up in Spanish at me. From inside the van, I could hear my protectees going nuts. I started to turn and head for the van, but my drunk friend was more fired up than ever. He tried to shove me.

"Don't touch me!" I growled.

He went on cursing, drunk and angry, until I grabbed and twisted his wrist and arm, hoping to create some distance and time between him and my protectees, who had finally gotten in the van and stayed put. I could see that his posse had started walking toward me. I spoke clearly and loudly enough for everyone to hear without yelling as I held him in the wristlock.

"Look, I'm not here to harm you. We're going to get into our van and get out of here, and that will be the end of this, OK?"

I didn't wait for him to answer. I let go, shoving him with some force. He stumbled backward, falling into the arms of his drunk buddies, and I swiftly closed the van's passenger door, finally closing off my protectees from these assholes, and did a quick jog to the front passenger seat of the van.

"You won't make it home alive tonight, *puta*!" he called out.

I kept my eye on him and my hand on my weapon as I stepped into the van.

"Go, go, go," I told the driver, who pulled away immediately. The OAS folks were going wild, yelling at each other and at me. I asked them to kindly shut the fuck up so I could focus as I went over what had just happened.

What *had* just happened? Would these guys follow us home? Was this incident a distraction to set us up for another surprise waiting along the route back to the hotel? Not soon enough, we arrived back at the hotel safely, and everyone wandered off to bed.

So now, two days later, across the table from me, our detail leader cleared his throat and said, "You are not going to like what we are about to tell you."

In my report, I had stated that I was concerned whether this was a random or a targeted incident. Did this individual know we were all affiliated with OAS?

As it turns out, the pirate and his drunk buddies were members of the Pantera Negra, or Black Panthers—a violent street gang known for dealing drugs and a long list of murders. Most likely, this had been a random incident. We'd been in the wrong place at the wrong time; some local gangsters had seen us as easy marks.

"How do you know that?" I asked.

"Well"—one guy turned to the other—"that's exactly why we called this meeting." Apparently, there were several policemen at the end of the block that night who saw what was going on, knew it involved Pantera Negra, and, well . . . they walked away. They feared the Pantera Negra would retaliate against them or, worse, kill them. What? Are you fucking kidding me? Hearing that made my blood boil. What kind of cops would leave foreigners—election observers, anybody for that matter—on their own in an altercation with gang members? I wondered whether the police were actually involved with the Pantera Negra somehow. For a moment, I just sat there, taking in this information. As it turned out, contrary to what we had thought, we couldn't rely on the police to help us, which meant the buck came to a screeching halt with me and Mike. No more trusting the Peruvian police.

Suddenly, I was responsible for what I knew in WFO would have been the work of six or seven agents. And though I was lucky, for the most part, to be among competent colleagues that I could learn from—with Mike as my partner in Peru and with other team members throughout my private protection career—what I had to learn, I was realizing, was *a lot*. What's more, trying to run a USSS-caliber mission without the million-dollar budget and personnel a massive federal agency provided was an exercise in futility. I could only depend on my training so much. At some point, I'd have to improvise.

This assignment required a lot of on-the-job adjustments, and it wasn't just because of the limits imposed by a smaller budget and smaller team than I was used to. It was also due to the somewhat unpredictable nature of the ambassador.

Within a few days of arriving and settling into the hotel, the ambassador told us he'd be up at 7:00 a.m. to get some exercise in the form of a long walk on the beach. Already my partner and I knew each other well enough that we didn't need to talk to know that accompanying the protectee for this task would fall into my wheelhouse, not Mike's. This meant that my day would begin at five in the morning, since I'd want to have my coffee and get the lay of the land to be ready in case the ambassador woke up early.

The next day, after finding a great coffee and breakfast spot, I jogged back to my room, got my running gear, my weapon, and other equipment squared away, and sat on the bed, with the sun from the beach streaming in through the terrace window and the room door wide open so I'd hear the sound of the ambassador opening his door. I wanted to be ready to greet him and let him know I had his back covered, but I knew that finding someone standing outside your door first thing in the morning can be a bit off-putting, even—or especially—when their job is to protect you. Besides, it was only six fifteen, and the ambassador didn't plan to be ready until seven. Of course, I was also realistic. Everybody struggles at times to pull themselves out of bed to work out, so I knew he might not hit seven on the dot.

Therefore when seven passed with no sight of the ambassador, I didn't think twice about it. But then seven thirty passed, and I was still perched on my bed watching the door. At seven forty-five, I started to get worried. Just then, the phone rang.

It was the ambassador. "No walk today. I'll see you at ten for the first meeting."

"OK, ambassador. Is everything OK?"

"Ten, Maribel," he said, then hung up.

I dialed Mike's room to let him know what was up.

"What time is it?" he said.

"Almost eight, 5-0." He wasn't scheduled to be on duty until that afternoon, so I understood why he didn't sound very happy to be talking to me at that hour. Still, I wanted to let him know what was up, just in case the ambassador changed his mind and called looking for me. I was already dressed, so I told Mike I'd be going out for a quick run, but I'd be back by nine in case the ambassador was ready early.

At ten sharp, I knocked on the ambassador's door, and he greeted me in his suit and tie. We spent the day going from political meetings to lunch to more meetings. It was a long day, and I could hardly blame him for not wanting to hit the beach to get some exercise in first thing. Later that evening when Mike and I debriefed back at the hotel, it made even more sense. After I walked Mike through the late start and the ambassador's meetings, he filled me in on the night before. They hadn't gotten in until the wee hours. The ambassador's time in Lima wasn't all business.

After the debrief, I went to my room and changed clothes, then met Mike back down in the lobby. We talked shop until the ambassador came downstairs—showered, clothes changed, and ready to head out for another night on the town.

Before leaving with Mike, the ambassador turned to me and said, "Maribel, are you sure you don't want to come out with us tonight?"

Mike was perfectly fine with working the night shift, but it was not my cup of tea nor, quite frankly, was it an appropriate environment for me to work. I had no desire to accompany our protectee into night-clubs and, as a female, keep watch while he drank cocktails, danced, and mingled with the other patrons.

"No, gracias, señor," I said. "That's very tempting, but I'll see you bright and early for our morning walk, right?" I tried not to roll my eyes too obviously.

"Seven o'clock, Maribel!" He was grinning and so was Mike as I bid them a good night.

This got to be the routine, both the promised—and rarely accomplished—walks on the beach in the morning and the ambassador's spirited evening outings. I didn't mind too much; I really enjoyed the early mornings by myself in Lima. Leaving the hotel and walking to different cafes for coffee and breakfast gave me an opportunity to talk with the locals and get a feel for what was going on in the neighborhood each morning, especially when I didn't have intelligence briefings to rely on. I learned quickly that locals are great sources of intelligence and that being friendly can prove extremely helpful. I never discussed what I was doing in Lima, but just by striking up conversation, I was able to create my own network of information.

One of the first locals I befriended was a waitress at my favorite coffee shop close to the hotel. Like most workers in Lima, Beatriz traveled far—two hours—using public transportation to come into the city to work because she could not afford to live in Lima proper; it was inconceivably expensive for her. In a country where the average monthly wage was sixty dollars at that time, an extra fifty cents or a dollar tip on a daily basis was a huge amount of money to her and next to nothing to me. Beatriz and others like her weren't immune to the violence of the Sendero Luminoso, which, to deter elections, would knock out electricity, put bombs on the buses headed into Lima, and threaten villagers.

Mike did his share of intelligence gathering too. He told me he had some CIA contacts, so I hoped that we'd get some kind of a warning if shit was about to hit the fan—a revolution, an air strike, another encounter with the Pantera Negra. I felt confident that if I were going to die in Peru, it would be because I was in the wrong place at the wrong time, not because some asshole wasn't happy with the OAS being in country. That might seem like a small comfort, but it helped to put things in perspective. Wrong place, wrong time doesn't mean much: it's how people die in Ypsilanti, Oslo, Beijing, and, yes, Lima, Peru.

The folks on the observation team were an interesting bunch. They held high-level positions in their respective countries and struck me as deeply committed to the OAS mission, despite the fact that the office received bomb threat after bomb threat. I knew that for many of the observers, having come from relatively poor countries, the OAS mission was an important opportunity. The OAS paid each observer a daily stipend, plus all of us were paid an extra one hundred dollars a day as "danger pay." That was a lot of money to me in those years, never mind to someone who came from a country where the economy was far less stable. After weeks of blackouts, bombings, and threats, these team members divulged their fears to me in conversation after conversation. I tried not to scare them, but I felt an obligation to be transparent about the situation they—all of us—were in.

I couldn't answer for them when they'd ask, "What am I doing here? Should I leave?" But when they asked, "Mary Beth, are you considering leaving?" I answered without hesitation: "I'll be here to complete the mission. As long as the OAS and the ambassador are here, I will be here."

The bomb threats proceeded unabated. One day, one came

in just as we were arriving with the ambassador to the high-rise that housed the OAS office, just twenty minutes from our hotel. Our observers had already been evacuated when we pulled up. I got out of the car and told Mike—who was with us on a fluke because he had some paperwork to sign at the office—to pack the ambassador up and take him back to the hotel. I then went to appraise the situation. The Peruvian national police were contemplating going in to search for a device—if there was one. They weren't sure if the threat was real or not, but they seemed pretty convinced. I did a quick head count—all observers were accounted for. Staffers did not always come into the office, so I could not be 100% sure if they were all outside and accounted for.

"Look," I told the observers, "go back to the hotel. Get away from this building."

I was piling them into cabs when one of the younger observers, a girl who worked for the OAS side by side with her uncle, ran up to me, crying.

"Maribel!" She was shaking. "They're not listening to me!" She pointed to the police. "Tio Alberto, he's not here!"

Shit.

"Are you sure he was here today?"

"Yes, yes, he's there!" She pointed at the third floor of the building, where the OAS offices were.

"OK. *Tranquila.* Don't worry." I took a last look around at the crowd, hoping to spot the uncle, but he wasn't anywhere to be seen. I headed over to the police, who were still debating the credibility of the threat.

"There's somebody, one of our staff, inside the building, third floor!" I said.

"We don't know if there's an explosive device inside, señora," one of them said.

"Yes, and one of my people is still inside!"

I was met with silence.

"Are any of you going to get him?" I asked.

"It's not safe."

Ok, roger that. I looked at the door to the building and then back to the crying girl. God damn it. I knew it wasn't my job to go into the building, but I didn't know if I could live with myself if the place blew up and this girl's uncle died after she'd asked for my help. I took a deep breath and jogged in, ignoring the police yelling at me.

No one was in the lobby.

I ran up to the office, taking the steps two, three at a time, trying not to think about how stupid it was to run toward a bomb threat.

"Alberto!" I called out.

There was no sign of anyone in any of the offices.

"Alberto, are you here?"

The conference room was empty. I was still panting, thinking about where he could be. My heart was racing, fully aware that with every second that went by the risk climbed.

"Alberto!"

I heard something, a click, and I held my breath. It was the lock to the bathroom. The door opened. Then, tentatively, Alberto stepped out.

"Alberto, let's go!"

"Maribel, is everything OK? Where is everybody?" he asked, looking around at the empty office.

"Now!" I grabbed his jacket and escorted him downstairs, quickly, and out the doors to his still-sobbing niece.

Alberto had been in the bathroom when the bomb threat was called in. Hearing the police announcements, he stayed where he was, fearing that he might find an attack, maybe even terrorists, awaiting him on the other side of the bathroom door. Once we were safely back at the hotel, Tio Alberto and I laughed about the incident, but his niece never did think it was funny.

After another mission that took us out of the city, I returned to Lima with the ambassador to find no fewer than a dozen messages from my mother waiting for me at the hotel. I called her back immediately, terrified that something had happened to my father.

"Mom, what's—"

"Are you okay? Are you okay? Oh, my God!" She was in more of a rush than I was.

"Mom . . . Mom, wait, wait, wait! What's going on?"

"There was a coup attempt in Lima, and they tried to take out President Fujimori! It's all over the news here." I had never heard her so desperate before.

"Mom, I swear to God, I'm fine. I don't even know what you're talking about." I was relieved that she wasn't calling to tell me some bad news. We had heard some rumblings from Lima on the road, but since we'd been back, things had been business as usual.

"You're lying to me." She was calmer now, but she sounded hurt.

"I am not. Honest, Mom. We haven't heard anything about a coup attempt. Plus, I haven't been anywhere near the capital for days." I was starting to get a little angry, too—not at her, but that something like this would have made news in the States and our management team hadn't bothered to let us know what was going on while we were out in the field. "Mom, I've been out in the countryside with the ambassador all day. Everything is fine here. Nothing happened, and if it did, we'd all be back in DC, or at least safe at the US embassy, quicker than you'd know. Now, I have to tell you about this helicopter ride I went on!"

I told her that I'd joined the OAS ambassador when he was invited to take a tour of the Lineas de Nazca, a series of giant geoglyphs stretched out over fifty miles of the Nazca Desert in southern Peru. The tour had to be done by helicopter because no humans are allowed to walk on the Nazca Lines in order to preserve this national treasure. As I finished my account of the trip, the lights in my hotel room flickered. I held my breath for a moment, worried that the call would get cut off.

"Where are you now?" My mom's voice came back over the line.

"I'm back at the hotel in Lima. It's really nice, actually. You would like it here, Mom. Great coffee, delicious food, and the beach is two blocks away."

In spite of the Sendero Luminoso's campaign of terror, the elections for a new legislature took place. Most important to me was that, aside from a few cases of altitude sickness, some food poisoning, and more than a few pisco sour hangovers, not one of the observers was hurt.

The entire eight-member security team contract was renewed for the upcoming municipal elections. We headed home for a couple of weeks for Christmas and then returned to Lima, with the same four team members working in the capital and the other four heading out to the already-established OAS offices around the country.

It was early January 1993, and the Sendero Luminoso had assassinated over a dozen mayoral candidates just since late December 1992. Several were murdered via drive-by gunfire, some at point-blank right in the heart of the towns they governed, and some by bombs detonated at their homes or offices. Because there were thousands of candidates running for mayoral and city council positions, it was impossible for Peru to provide security for all of them. Over one hundred candidates resigned in fear.

During the second half of the mission in Peru, more of my time was spent in the countryside away from Lima, where the ambassador met with election officials and candidates, dealt with anti-government factions in the hopes of helping to broker ceasefires, and investigated claims of election fraud. Though I was on my guard as the sole agent protecting the ambassador during these day trips, I felt lucky to see so much of Peru's incredible natural beauty, rich culture, and diverse people. It's a place full of history, physical grace, and natural wonders, like Machu Picchu, the floating Uros Islands on Lake Titicaca, and the unspoiled, undeveloped beaches of Lima. The expansive landscape was unexpected, as were the many llama farms where indigenous women made beautiful wool sweaters, scarves, and blankets. Peruvians are a fascinating multiethnic people. Although the official language is Spanish, I was surprised to learn that approximately 15 percent of the population only spoke Quechua, the main language of the Incan Empire. I loved the food in Peru, the diversity of the neighborhoods of Lima, and the warmth of the people throughout the country.

The Floating Uros Islands on Lake Titicaca, Peru, 1992

During my five months in Peru, I learned that being an exceptional protection agent in a developing country entailed not only improvisation but also a sincere respect for the local language and culture. It meant that I had to do as much as possible with the few resources I had—one other American security agent, two Peruvian security drivers, two vehicles, and two radios. I became a better advance agent. After all, I had to plan as much as I could prior to traveling anywhere because we usually wound up with no functioning means of communication whenever we ventured outside the main cities.

I got better at being diplomatic, even when the people who were supposed to be helping me were the ones putting up the roadblocks. That meant that I had to think and work outside the box and enlist the cooperation of people I hoped I could trust, including airport security, police and military officers, hotel and restaurant staff, OAS observers, and even my protectee.

I also had to learn the importance of protecting a protectee from himself. After all, protecting a client from embarrassment is the second most important responsibility of a protection agent.

Just a few days before the municipal election, in a small town near Lima, after a very long morning meeting, our group, which included five observers and the ambassador, was invited to lunch. This lunch turned out to be an almost six-hour affair, with many courses of food and plenty of wine, beer, and liquor. The meeting had been successful on both sides, so the mood was festive from the start. One of our observers started the celebration off with a toast: "To fair elections!" A cheer went up as the first of many rounds was consumed.

The ambassador looked over at me and said, "Maribel, you have to relax and enjoy this lunch too—have a drink!"

I just smiled, said thank you, and declined. I was working, so of course I didn't drink, but after weeks of tension and the elections just around the corner, I understood their need to unwind.

The ambassador was a lively drunk, and with each alcoholic beverage, he became more entertaining. He kept trying to get me to "relax and have a drink," which became a little annoying after the third or fourth attempt. After two hours at this lunch, he started to become a little suggestive. I knew it was the alcohol talking and just blew him off. At hour five, with no sign of the party slowing down, the ambassador was slurring his words and sharing inappropriate stories. I knew it was time to go.

"Maribel, I . . . I have to piss," he said.

I simply nodded. *Gee, thanks for the update*, I thought to myself.

When he got up to head to the bathroom, I moved to the center of the room and spoke quickly.

"Thank you, everyone, for your hospitality. It's getting late"—it was 5:00 p.m.—"and the ambassador has a meeting back in Lima."

As I radioed the driver of our vehicle, I walked briskly over to the men's room and stood guard. When the ambassador emerged, I escorted him to our vehicle.

"Maribel, where are we going? I have to . . ." he started to ask, a little confused and still disheveled, as I helped him into the back seat of the car and quickly jumped into the front passenger side, letting the driver know we were heading back to the hotel. Given the opportunity, I knew the ambassador would try to get back to the lunch and keep the party going a little longer, so I started talking in an effort to distract him.

"Ambassador, I was thinking, the next time we go for a walk in the morning, maybe we should try a new route. The beach is nice, but it's good to change up our routine, don't you think?"

The ambassador didn't respond. He'd fallen asleep almost the instant I had buckled him in.

The day before the municipal elections, at noon on a business day, in the posh neighborhood of La Molina, which was approximately ten miles from our hotel, a powerful car bomb went off outside of the Peruvian headquarters of IBM. The car was loaded with nearly seven hundred pounds of ammonium nitrate. IBM was reportedly targeted for providing assistance to the government of Peru in the form of tallying votes. Fifteen people were wounded, and the IBM facility and many other nearby buildings, including fifty homes in the neighborhood, sustained heavy damage. I felt like I was in a war zone where the lines of battle were invisible and ever-shifting. Once again, I sent up a silent prayer of gratitude for the safety of those people in my charge. If success was the outcome of luck and preparation, I knew I had the latter point covered, but coming to terms with my inability to control the unexpected would be a lifelong project.

Most of Lima was closed the day of elections: shop owners feared retaliation, and because much of the public transportation was not operating, workers could not get into the city anyway. Buses burned in the streets, the Sendero Luminoso's grim warning to stay away from the polls.

The scare tactic worked. Voter turnout was historically low. Fujimori, meanwhile, succeeded with his own brand of fear-mongering for another seven years before decamping to Japan amid accusations of corruption and widespread human rights abuses. It would take another seven years before he would finally be extradited back to Peru to stand trial. By then, I had long shaken off the tensions of my time in troubled Lima. The Peruvian people were, however, just confronting a ghost of those violent months, one that had continued to haunt them, even from halfway around the world.

CHAPTER
6

From where we stood in the dim, cobwebbed tunnel, I could smell water in the distance. Somewhere ahead of us, drunken-sounding men were shouting at each other in what sounded like French. I smelled something sharp and metallic in the air—maybe gunpowder? The three young girls in my charge crowded around me as a surge of people pressed us forward. One of the girls took my hand, her small palm clammy and warm. *How frightened is she?* I wondered. Just as we rounded a dark corner, a tiny flashlight clicked on behind us. Ken Dart was getting back to his reading.

"Daddy, how much longer?" one of his daughters asked him, breaking his laser-like focus on the report that he had pulled from his ever-present briefcase.

"Not too long, now, honey. This is all part of the experience," Ken responded, then went back to his reading.

"Just be patient, sweetie," Jan, Ken's wife, responded. "We'll get to the front of the line soon enough."

"But I am dying to ride Pirates of the Caribbean," Corey said.

You and everyone else, little one, I thought. Judging by the snail's pace of our progress toward the boat that would send us sailing past shipwrecks and dungeons, we were waiting for one of the most popular rides at Euro Disney. The girls, I could tell, were starting to tire at the tail end of an action-packed trip to Paris that had so far included a tour of Versailles, visits to Notre Dame and the Louvre, sunny afternoons in oh-so-French parks and gardens, and lunches at quaint cafes. Their father, on the other hand, never seemed to lose steam, at least when it came to working, and neither pirates nor patisseries could stop him from making his way through the piles of paperwork that seemed to accompany him everywhere.

Pick up any Styrofoam cup and you will most likely see one of three brands on the bottom: Solo, Sweetheart, or Dart. It's a mystery, at least to me, where the first two got their names, but I can tell you that the third company, Dart, is named for the family that started it. William A. Dart graduated from the University of Michigan in the late 1950s with not one but three degrees: metallurgy, mathematics, and engineering. Dart was convinced the future was in plastics, and after a short stint with DuPont, he began experimenting with and perfecting a molding process for expanded polystyrene (EPS), Styrofoam to you and me. In 1960, Dart Container Corporation was born, and that same year, they began selling insulated foam cups. This innovation, and the company's subsequent success, made the family very wealthy. It was Ken Dart, one of William's three sons, who brazenly hoisted the family from millionaire to billionaire status. In the early 1990s, he had diversified—and greatly expanded—the family's wealth through various investments and business dealings around the globe. It was one of these investments—or, more precisely, the alleged frightening fallout from it going south—that had led to me joining the family on their European vacation.

In May 1994, while I was living in Washington, DC, and in the midst of working an extremely intense investigation, I received a call from a guy named Jay. He introduced himself and said he'd gotten my name from a mutual friend who had highly recommended me for an executive protection position he needed to fill in Sarasota, Florida. He told me next to nothing about the job, but what he did offer—a one-month contract with the option to renew, assuming I was a good fit for the position—was enough to entice me to accept. I mean, who could say no to a month of running on the beach, eating fresh seafood, and soaking up the sun?

I packed my bags, tossed them in the back of the beautiful soft-top Jeep Wrangler I had just purchased, and headed south. Though I had never worked in a private protection capacity for a family as wealthy as the Darts, Jay's call had come at just the right time. I desperately needed a change of scenery, and the investigation I'd been working was enough to make my head spin. I found a great apartment just over the bridge from Siesta Key Beach, which is known for its beautiful white sand and throngs of bikini-clad spring breakers. From my front door, it was just over a quarter mile to the ocean, and what better way for a running junkie to destress than by tracing a route to the seashore every morning?

What I quickly discovered about working with private families, as opposed to working with ambassadors and politicians, is that hiring someone with my skill set is rarely a preventative security measure. It usually takes an incident to scare families into putting together a security team. This was the case for the Vegas mogul, Steve Wynn, whose twenty-six-year-old daughter, Kevyn, was kidnapped from her home in 1993 and found bound and gagged in the trunk of her car after Wynn paid her abductors a ransom of $1.45 million. Prior to this incident, Steve Wynn had been adamantly opposed to having an overt and full-on security detail. After this incident, he moved his entire family to a newly built compound that was as secure as Fort Knox, and he expanded his own detail and hired an impressive security team. This was also the case for the Darts, though thankfully their children were not expressly targeted.

On September 9, 1993, a home that Ken Dart was having built for his family in an upscale Sarasota neighborhood burned to the ground. After ascertaining that the home had been doused with diesel fuel and set ablaze, fire investigators ruled that this was a case of arson. Because the house was still under construction, no one was in the home, and, fortunately, no one was hurt.

Ken and his wife, Jan, immediately hired contract security agents to protect their family. At the time, there were several theories about who the arsonists might be, and the Darts did not want to take any (more) risks. Once things settled down, a few months after the arson, Ken and his wife acknowledged that, even though they didn't welcome it, having physical protection teams in their lives was necessary. Their wealth and the public profile it resulted in had changed their lives forever, and threats, whether veiled or blatant, would always exist. Hence, they decided to shift away from the contracted protection agents they had been using to a more permanent, in-house team. In doing this, the Darts saved a tremendous amount of money and were able to maintain more consistency and create a more insulated wall of privacy and protection. Rather than having a constantly changing cast rotating in and out of their lives, the family would see the same set of familiar faces. They would have two teams of security, named Blue and Gold, with each working a three-week rotation, usually followed by three weeks of downtime.

The afternoon I arrived in Sarasota, I met the mission's "front office"—that is, the director and assistant director of the Dart family protection detail, who worked out of the corporate office in the quaint downtown area. Jay was older and had been one of the first agents sent by the DC security firm the Dart family had hired right after the fire. When the family decided to create an in-house security company, rather than outsource it, Jay transitioned into the role of director. Don, the assistant director, was a former Army Criminal Investigative Division Special Agent.

Jay, I knew, had never been a detail leader before, and he had certainly never been a director of security. The word on the street was that he was okay to work with as a team member but nothing to write home about. He was also known to be a bit of a suck-up with protectees, so when the Dart family decided to create an in-house security company, Jay was right there drooling at Ken Dart's feet. It worked out well for him, but I had my doubts about his lack of experience managing people and his reputation as anything but a team player. Don, however, was someone I got along well with; I thought he had a great sense of humor and a solid work ethic.

Seated across a conference table from Jay and Don, I answered their questions about my previous protection training and experience. They already had my resume, and I knew they had spoken with various references. It wasn't like they were going to send me packing unless I screwed up and said something really stupid, which, thank you yet again, Larry Wilkas, wasn't going to happen. I had a solid background, excellent training, and plenty of experience in the field. Jay and Don liked my pedigree; they loved the idea of a former Secret Service agent joining the team they had created and were managing.

Jay leaned back in his chair and spun his pen between his thumb and index finger. "If I'm being completely honest with you, Mary Beth, I need to tell you that you'll probably notice some things are a bit— how should I put this—off with your team, the Blue Team. They're good, but they're not great. Definitely not your caliber."

His comment caught me off guard, and I didn't like his confidential, insider tone. We'd just met. Plus, if there was an issue with the team, wasn't it Jay's job to resolve it?

"What Jay is saying, Mary Beth, is that we think you'd be wise to simply do your job and not make any waves with them for now." Don made a steeple with his hands on the table and smiled. "Give it a little time, and it'll work out well for you."

Now I was really thrown. What the hell was he talking about? "I'm sorry. I'm not understanding."

"We're hoping to put you in charge of Blue Team," Jay clarified.

"Oh. OK. . . . Interesting. Got it." Although many other agents sitting in my chair would have been drooling at this point, I was really turned off. What I was honestly thinking in that moment was, *What kind of bullshit, backstabbing operation were they running here?* However, I maintained my poker face and said, "The Darts haven't even met me yet."

Jay and Don reassured me the family would love me, and then they briefed me on the setup of the detail: team division, schedule, command post operations, training opportunities, and, of course, the family itself. We eventually got to the reason the Darts needed a protection team in the first place: someone had burned down their house.

There were several working theories about who had started the fire, ranging from bored, pyromaniac teenagers, to Ken's estranged older brother, Tom, who claimed he had been swindled of billions by Ken and his family members, to a disgruntled group of Brazilian bankers. This last scheme possessed all the elements of a great spy novel—a mysterious ultra-wealthy executive, international intrigue, and greed—and though the arson was never solved, this was the explanation presented to me as the most likely when I arrived in Sarasota.

I'll share the broad strokes with you: In the early 1990s, under the auspices of Dart Management, a so-called "vulture fund," Ken Dart purchased four percent of Brazil's $35 billion debt for approximately $375 million. As they attempted to restructure their debt, the Brazilian government tried to negotiate with Ken Dart to buy back the share he had purchased. Allegedly, all other debt owners had already successfully negotiated with Brazil. Dart, however, consistently scuttled their efforts, making him the only standout to resolution, supposedly enraging the group of Brazilian bankers working tirelessly on their nation's behalf. Dart's strategy paid off: by 1994, Ken's measly four percent stake was worth $980 million, generating a cool $600 million in profit for his company.

Jay cleared his throat to make way for the most critical piece of information yet: they had determined that Brazil posed a clear international threat to Ken and his family, and they were certain it was the

Brazilians who were responsible for the arson of the Dart family home.

I was waiting for the "just kidding" to come out of Jay's mouth, but it didn't happen. Sure, Ken had made more than a few enemies in his line of work, but come on. Seriously? I looked over at Don to register his facial expression and determine whether he, like me, thought this was total bullshit, but he just sat dutifully next to Jay, nodding.

Listen, I may not be the world's most informed individual, but I had been in this business long enough, traveled enough, and read enough newspapers and intelligence reports to know that pissed-off Brazilian bankers did not make a habit of sending thugs to Sarasota, Florida, to set houses on fire. A seed of distrust cracked open inside me. Either these guys had seen too many movies, or they had fabricated this tale to frighten the Darts and keep themselves gainfully employed. Either way, I knew a big red flag when I saw one, and this one was waving like a beauty pageant winner. Still, I was beyond curious to find out what the hell was going on here.

No matter their skill or experience, protection agents are a less-than-ideal presence in any family's world. Regardless of how wealthy or famous people are, most of them want to live a "normal" life. That's hard to do when you have armed professionals following you around twenty-four hours a day, seven days a week. People in my position know all kinds of embarrassing, intimate details about our protectees, and even in the name of security, that level of transparency can be hard to accept. The older members of the Dart family, Ken's parents in particular, viewed me and my colleagues skeptically; as far as they were concerned, we were just a drain on their hard-earned family money. And while I believe it was money well spent, I should note that—without naming names—there are certain high-profile people in my industry who have made millions by putting the fear of God into the rich and powerful and then selling them on astronomically priced security packages. It happens. A lot.

The transition might have been the hardest on Jan. Before she and Ken decided to hire a protection team, she had been living a very low-key life, driving her kids to school in a minivan, doing her daily errands around town, and going from place to place on her own schedule, at her pace, getting things done in whatever order she wanted. From one day to the next, Jan lost nearly all control of her daily routines, as well as her daughters'. Her security team needed to know her schedule, as we would be driving her to appointments, lunch with her friends, the grocery store—everywhere. She was also asked for each of her daughter's schedules, as well as who their friends were and where they lived, where they tended to spend their free time, and their medical histories. Other people in her life—say, her cleaning lady—suddenly came under scrutiny, as we had to conduct background investigations on everyone in the Darts' inner circle.

In executive protection, trust is hugely important, but it's also essential for a protection agent to understand the workplace culture (that workplace being the protectee's home and business) and expectations. This is one reason a trial period, whether it's explicitly stated or not, is pretty much a given for every new agent on a protection detail. You do not just walk into an individual's life, hang out on their property, learn a tremendous amount of personal information about them, and hop into their vehicles and drive them around town without them really scrutinizing whether they like you, believe you fit in, and believe they can trust you. This is particularly true when there are children involved.

I have heard of protection agents being let go from security teams because of the color of their hair, because they were not cultured enough, and because they dressed better than the client and the client was none too pleased. This is a commonsense rule of executive protection: never, ever outdress your client. On the flip side, I've worked with people who were spoken to because their attire was a bit sloppy or inappropriate for the job. In one particular case, the detail leader gently admonished a female agent to me because her attire was a bit drab, saying that word had come down from "above." This agent was actually given a nice stipend to upgrade her wardrobe, which was testament to the kindness of the family we were protecting, and I was asked to go with her to help her shop. Talk about awkward.

That said, it's important to maintain a healthy distance from the people you're protecting. Say, one day a CEO comes up to you and says, "Oh, hey, how are you?" Some people make the mistake of thinking these kinds of exchanges break down a barrier between protector and protectee—that you're suddenly friends. Listen closely: *They are not your friends.* This is rule number one in the executive protection handbook. You have a job to do—stay focused. This comes up in private sector training all the time, particularly in the Hollywood scene. I can't tell you how many starstruck protective agents have said to me, "So-and-so is going to read my script, and I'm gonna star in the movie." Tell you what: I'll keep watching the Oscars every year, but until I see one of these agents glide across the stage decked out in Armani, I'll maintain that they're a tad delusional.

Fitting in with a family's culture sometimes has little to do with an agent's ability to do his or her work. A British agent I met who worked for Robert Dart, Ken's brother, was fired because he was seen picking his teeth with a fork while working a family country club event. He was a good agent, but that's just the way it goes in the world of executive protection. You could be one of the most well-known and well-respected agents around, but that does not mean you will fit in with every client. I have known agents that are great on high-threat missions, but they don't adapt well to protecting individuals or families. I have also known protection agents who only do well with the Hollywood-type clients and would never make it on some of the higher-threat assignments. Just like every other human being, every protection agent has unique strengths and weaknesses.

As my one-month trial period rolled out, I got to know the streets of Sarasota, the routes most frequently traveled by the family, many of the alternate routes, and the back roads. I learned the restaurants the family most frequented, the stores they most often visited, and the places they spent most of their leisure time. I studied the Sarasota–Bradenton International Airport, specifically the arrival and departure routines of Ken, who was a very frequent flyer. I not only familiarized myself with his daughters' daily routines—departure and pick-up times, drop-off locations, extracurricular schedules, and so on—but I also researched the private school they attended, assessing all the key (and not so key) people there.

The first day, when I was driving the girls to school with one of my teammates, the oldest daughter, Kelly, asked me, "Were you *really* a Secret Service agent?" When I told her that I had been, Kristen, the youngest daughter, said, "What's a Secret Service agent?" I smiled and told her, "They're the people who protect the president of the United States and wear cool sunglasses." "Oh!" she said. "I know who they are, I saw them on TV!" They were both glad to have another female around, as so many members of the Dart staff and security team were male.

Perhaps most importantly during this initial trial period, I began to get to know the people—my Blue Team members, the command post agents, and, of course, the family. Naturally, the reverse was also true; they were all getting to know me and deciding whether I would survive the cut, so to speak. Knowing I was being evaluated on a day-to-day basis could be intense, never mind annoying, but I would question the protectee or team leader who didn't look closely at the people they hired. A lot of executive protection contracting happens via word-of-mouth and referrals, which means, without creating an explicit paper trail, asking around about someone's previous positions is a necessary part of the process if you're going to catch the bullshitters and frauds. And, holy shit, does this industry have their fair share of them. It's not uncommon for a few years of military experience to get bumped up to Special Forces, or Navy SEAL, or something else equally impressive but just as untrue.

Luckily for me, the Dart family was fantastic—down to earth, easy to work with, and just good people. Jan was always warm and gracious; the three girls were sweet, smart, and funny; and Ken was kind and curious. If you observed their day-to-day habits, you'd never know they were billionaires. They shopped at Target, ate at Boston Market, and drove an American-made minivan. As my assignment went on, I got to know the personalities of my protectees: their habits, their moods, their communication styles, their quirks, their likes and dislikes. This is the nature of the protection game—if you want to be good at the job, that is. All games have rules, and once you learn them, you can create and master your own strategies to succeed. One of my best strategies with families was to treat them like my own, without the hair pulling and name calling, of course. In other words, treat them like normal people. The Darts and I gelled well together, and it did not take long for me to feel that the family not only trusted me but that they wanted me to join the Blue Team on a more permanent basis. I couldn't have predicted at the time that this would turn out to be both a blessing and a curse.

As far as my "good-but-not-great" team members went, we got along extremely well, pretty much from day one. From Jay and Don's descriptions, I had expected to be working with the Keystone Cops of the executive protection world, but in fact the members of my team were fun, welcoming, and pretty easygoing about the possibility that I might be joining their team for a month or even permanently. Vern, the team leader, had led executive protection teams in the past. I trusted him immediately and could not understand why the front office would want to replace him. He was organized, had created and manualized a standard operating procedure, was on top of the family's schedules, knew the family's personalities and profiles, and was impressively level-headed. Every member of the family, Ken included, adored him.

Bill, whom we called Billy, was one of the funniest people I had ever met. Besides having a great personality, Billy was a great protection agent. He'd grown up as a neighborhood tough guy in Brooklyn, and as a young man, he had taken up boxing. Not only was he in great shape, he was extremely disciplined and could be super focused.

In fact, not only were all four of my teammates competent, each person had strengths that collectively made us a unique and very strong team. Two of the guys were beyond hilarious and fun to work with. I often dragged a couple of my teammates on my morning beach runs. Almost unfailingly, they'd whine about the humidity, complain that they were hungry, and wonder why I had to run so many miles in the sand. They paid me back in the weight room at the gym. Doing the same routines they did was brutal, only I never complained—hell, I'd rather pull a muscle to keep up with them than complain or give up. Remember, never let them see you sweat! Needless to say, between keeping up with my athletic teammates and taking advantage of the Sarasota sunshine, I stayed in great shape.

"Come on, girls," I called back through the small but spacious private jet. "Let's hustle."

The Dart daughters gathered their things and clambered to the jet door, and we all made our way off the plane. We'd just landed on Grand Cayman, and there were no pirates in sight, just intoxicating Caribbean air and the prospect of a weekend spent swimming; eating sweet, succulent shrimp; and doing my job.

While I was based in Sarasota with Jan and the girls, Ken split his time between Florida and Grand Cayman. In order to take advantage of Grand Cayman's friendlier tax laws, the scion of the Dart family had given up his US citizenship, which meant Ken could only spend a certain number of days each year on US soil. His kids, however, had many more years of school to complete stateside, so, for the time being, the Dart family shuttled back and forth between two gorgeous locales.

Fortunately, Ken had the means, by way of private aircrafts, to accommodate his unique transportation requirement at any hour of any day. He flew from Grand Cayman to Sarasota in his private plane. Once on the ground, he transferred from his plane to his private helicopter, which flew him from the Sarasota airport to his family's nearby property. Ken's wife and daughters lived in a modest home on a large piece of land. In fact, there was enough acreage that the Darts were able to get approval from the Federal Aviation Administration (FAA) to create an official landing zone for his helicopter arrivals. As you can imagine, this was a controversial project as far as the locals were concerned. But the FAA approved the landing zone, and when it came to family, nothing could stop Ken from seeing his, not even irate neighbors.

Working for the Darts entailed odd hours that went along with the laws Ken had to abide by as an expat. Because the number of days Ken was allowed to spend in the United States was limited each year, he was careful not to burn that precious time unnecessarily. That meant his arrivals into the United States occurred just after midnight on Friday nights, and his departures out of the United States took place just before midnight on Sundays. This way Ken used up just two days instead of three or four. For the protection team, this translated to late nights on Fridays and Sundays. Sayonara, social life!

Although Ken visited Sarasota on many weekends, his family often packed up and escaped to Grand Cayman to visit him as well. And why wouldn't they? The family had purchased an entire two-floor beachfront hotel, which they had gutted and remodeled, creating a beautiful home away from home. During my first weekend working with the family, just before summer break officially began for the Dart girls, we all traveled to Grand Cayman Island—Jan, the girls, my team members, and me. It was not a bad way to spend a weekend, that's for sure. People on Grand Cayman Island knew the Darts, but the Darts didn't make themselves conspicuous. Every so often, a restaurant owner said hello to Ken, but it was more courteous than fawning. Ken was always pleasant in return. In eight months of working with the family, I don't recall ever seeing Ken not smiling at or saying a kind word to the people he met.

"Everyone, I'd like you to meet Mary Beth," Ken said, introducing me that first weekend in Grand Cayman to my colleagues there, the protection agents and command post personnel of the other Blue Team. During our visits to Grand Cayman, we worked alongside Ken's Blue security team. They were the complement to our Florida-based Blue Team, meaning they were on the same rotation schedule we were. When we were on the job, working our rotations with the family up in Sarasota, they were working the same rotation in Grand Cayman with Ken.

After I met this other team, assessed their setup, and chatted for a bit, Ken led me out of the command post to a deck overlooking the water. The color of the Caribbean was stunning, and I privately bookmarked the spot to return to off-duty sometime in the future. Once outside, Ken welcomed me to the team and thanked me for joining it. I let him know that I was glad to be working with his family.

Toward the end of the weekend, as we were wrapping things up for the evening, Ken asked me if I had a few minutes. "Of course," I said. I let my teammates know I would meet them back at our hotel as I jogged upstairs to Ken's office.

After asking how the weekend had been, he said, "Listen, Mary Beth, I know you haven't been with us for very long, but I want you to know I'm all ears if you have suggestions for how to tighten up security around here. My family means the world to me, and I'll do what it takes to keep them safe."

"Of course," I responded. There was an awkward silence, and I realized Ken was waiting for a critique of his current security team's practices. "You want to know what I think?"

"I would. Your honest opinion." Ken's face was as placid as ever, but my blood pressure instantly spiked. I wondered whether he was testing what kind of team player I was. Did he expect me to bad-mouth his team of three protection agents? Expose any imperfections I saw in their operations or those of the command post? Reveal any personal issues I had with them?

I knew, thanks to the grapevine, that the three members of Ken's Grand Cayman protection team, the Blue Team, had worked together for several years protecting former Secretary of State and National Security Advisor Henry Kissinger. This experience meant they knew each other's strengths and weaknesses, work styles, personalities, and temperaments well. It could take months for a team to gel, and even in my brief time with Ken's Grand Cayman guys, it was clear they ran a tight, unified ship. I couldn't say the same for Jay and Don, the knuckleheads back in the front office who had no business running a detail, but, hoping there might in the future be a better time and place to share my concerns, I bit my tongue.

"In all honesty, Ken, you have a solid group of protection and command post agents on the ground here," I told him. "I think you're in very good hands."

Ken smiled, nodded, and thanked me. Whew. Bullet dodged.

As I was getting settled into my second rotation, Don left the job abruptly, without saying goodbye to anyone. No one knew the reason, though there were plenty of rumors. I wondered if Don had stood up to Jay about something and lost. It was a shame, as Don was far more qualified to be the director of security—he had significantly more experience and integrity than Jay did.

Paco, a member of the Dart family's Grand Cayman Gold Team and—I had realized—Jay's informant, was tapped to replace Don. He was neither well-liked nor well-respected, a suck-up of the worst kind, who, if that weren't enough, thought himself quite the Lothario. He never failed to flirt with the female members of the team, and few trusted him. That Paco was rewarded with a promotion for diming out his teammates, mostly for things that did not even happen, sent another tremor through the already fracturing sense of morale among the Dart protection team.

Shortly after taking on his new role, Paco casually called me into the downtown office for a meeting. It was clear that he and Jay were frustrated by the Blue Team's autonomy and the fact that the Dart family preferred the Blue Team over the Gold Team. We all knew this; the Darts had actually scheduled their European vacation around the Blue Team's availability and had rejected Jay's suggestion that the Gold Team go instead. Jay and Paco thought two troublemakers—well, troublemakers in their power-hungry minds—Vern and Billy, were to blame for the unsatisfactory balance of power. As the meeting started, Paco got right down to business. He laid out how I would soon take over Blue Team and how things would change once I was in charge. He didn't stop there. Seeing as my "good-but-not-great" teammates weren't the most qualified agents out there, I should report any less-than-professional behavior to them. They were asking me to serve as their snitch, their canary, their informant. Of course, there was no way in hell I was going to do that. That they even assumed I would was insulting. Keeping a poker face was next to impossible, but I managed.

As stunned as I was in the moment, I also felt a twinge of regret. Even then, I could see that my time with a family I admired and enjoyed working for would not last. It was clear that the front office was determined to break up our team and get rid of our two best agents. With Vern and Billy gone, I would be reporting directly to the two people I had the least respect for on this mission. Plus, this was such a far cry from the standard of professionalism I had learned in the Secret Service that there was no way I could stay on, even if I wanted to, under this kind of leadership. If I didn't pull myself out of this shit-smelling quicksand of gossip, spite, and power-mongering soon, it would suck me down. Before long, I would offer my resignation, but I wasn't giving up just yet.

The Dart family European vacation moved on from France to the great city of London. We stayed in a beautiful hotel in the Knightsbridge neighborhood, close to Harrods, Buckingham Palace, and several museums. For me, the best part of staying in Knightsbridge was the proximity to Hyde Park, Kensington Gardens, and Green Park. I could not have asked for better running routes.

Having lived in Spain for almost four years, I had been to Paris and London several times, but traveling with the Darts was a totally different experience. In my younger days, I'd carried what I could in a backpack, crashed in hostels, and survived on whatever meal I could put together from the local market, usually some combination of baguette, cheese, tomatoes, and cookies. It was a little weird at first to be in a city I knew well but in a hotel with a doorman, 24-hour front desk attendants, and room service. To be honest, it took a bit of time to get used to.

About three minutes.

Okay, maybe four.

We set up a command post in a room next to the family's suite at the hotel. It was not your usual command post but rather a pared-down version with a monitor to observe the feed from the few cameras we'd set up in the hall, radio and phone chargers, extra radios, two large dry-erase boards, various maps of London, tourist information, and a couple of refrigerators for the agents to put food and drinks in.

After just one day of moving around London with the family, we all agreed there were too many protection agents traveling with the Darts. Even with two agents back at the command post and two agents going ahead to do advance work, that still left four agents crisscrossing the city with Ken, Jan, and the girls. Plus, once we arrived at a planned stop, the advance agents became part of the protection team. As a result, we stuck out like sore thumbs—not good.

Our team leader, Vern, in his infinite wisdom, divided our team of five as follows: him, then two sets of two agents. Each day, one pair of agents worked with him and the family while the other pair had down time. So, first I'm forced to stay in a posh hotel, and now I have to take a paid vacation every other day? Brutal. It was trips like this that made me think twice when the time came to make the decision to move on.

Billy, the other half of my duo, made a pact with me: on one of our days off, we'd take turns deciding what to do in the city. We toured

Harrod's together—my pick—then headed to the Harley Davidson store—his pick. After snagging a few T-shirts there, he turned to me: "Okay, it's your fucking turn. What's next?" I didn't have to think twice.

When we arrived at the Savoy Hotel for high tea, the doorman stopped us at the entrance. "Excuse me. May I help you?"

Billy, who was built like a brick shithouse and had made me swear to never tell a soul what we were about to do, lest it ruin his reputation, said in his classic Brooklyn accent, "Yeah, we're goin' to high tea." I half expected Billy to ask, "What's it to you, you mutt?" But he behaved himself.

"Well, sir," said the doorman, "I'm terribly sorry, but you cannot enter the hotel like that."

I could sense Billy's hackles go up instantaneously. "What do you mean, like this?"

"You see, sir, we have a dress code. The Savoy does not allow people wearing blue jeans to attend high tea."

"Are you fuckin' kiddin' me?" It was classic Billy, and I burst out laughing.

The doorman's eyes looked like they would pop out of his well-bred head. "Indeed, I am not, sir."

"You're fuckin' serious? We can't have high tea here because we're wearin' jeans?"

Clearing his throat, the doorman stiffly stated his message of earlier: "We have a dress code for high tea, sir. I am most sorry."

Having lost the blue jean battle, we wound up returning to our hotel for high tea, which, seeing as it had been Princess Diana's favorite spot for high tea, was nothing to scoff at. And, brace yourself, they allowed us to wear jeans. It was quite a sight to see, Billy stuffed into a too-small chair eating too-small sandwiches and sipping tea from a delicate cup. After the humiliation—or hilarity, depending on your point of view—of our ordeal at the Savoy, Billy, recognizing he looked just as out of his element as he felt, laughed harder than I did.

"Girls," Jan called. "You know the deal: stay where Mary Beth can see you."

Two of the Dart daughters had just gone back in the water for the fourth time that afternoon, and the youngest, Kristen, was drying off on a chair beside her mom. Two of my colleagues were in the water, where they could see and quickly swim to the girls if necessary. As Jan went back to her book, I scanned the horizon, the beach, and back, over and over. What a view. The bad situation in the front office was getting worse by the day, and I sensed my time with the Darts was drawing to a close. When it did, some other protective agent would be in my place enjoying the scene in front of me, but I wondered if they'd form the same close bond with the family I had. When, after eight months on the job, I offered my resignation—a day after Vern and a week after Billy—and explained that the team leadership had become untenable, Jan cried and said, "Not you too, Mary Beth."

But that day, the ocean was, as it was so many days in Grand Cayman, a gorgeous, glittering blue. No matter how beautiful though, a large body of water is a vulnerable place for anyone, all the more so for a billionaire's daughters. I wasn't worried about the girls' swimming skills so much as how quickly I could reach them if someone—or several someones—tried to abduct them. What was the likelihood I could outswim a jet ski? Slim to none, but then again, how likely was it that someone would try something so stupid? The island was seventy-six square miles—not much room to hide. On a jet ski or dinghy, they could maybe get to Cuba. If they were exceptionally stupid, they might set their sights on the US.

I took a breath and refocused on more likely possibilities. There was no shortage of those.

All beaches on the island were, by law, public. Nobody—not private residences, not hotels, not restaurants—was allowed to prohibit anyone from enjoying even a single inch of the beach. As a result, there wasn't much I could do to prevent people from accessing the beach in front of the Darts' oceanfront home. I was allowed, however, to prohibit people from walking through the actual physical property to get to the road because private property was just that—private. Hence, every so often, I got to say to a random tourist, with a big smile on my face, "I'm sorry, this is private property. You'll have to walk around another way."

"Mama?" Kristen asked. Her damp hair was still dripping on the towel wrapped up around her as she curled up to her mother on a beach chair.

"Yes, my love?" Jan replied, putting her book down and stroking her daughter's head. The sun, I could tell, was starting to make the girl sleepy.

"Will you ever be able to drive us places again?"

Jan, an extremely wealthy woman wearing a bathing suit she'd found on a rack at Target, stiffened beneath her drowsy child. She looked up at me. From behind my sunglasses, I caught a flash of anguish on her face.

"Of course, honey. Someday."

CHAPTER
7

PORT-AU-PRINCE, HAITI

1995

"Heads up!" More than a few items in the armored SUV went flying as the driver slammed on the brakes, but a moment's notice was all I needed to brace myself in the back seat and keep my Uzi in position, pointed out the window.

"What the fuck, Jake?"

"Get used to it, Wilkas. Driving in Port-au-Prince is a regular demolition derby."

"No shit. Can't wait for my turn. Try to get us there in one piece!"

"You know I will," he said, looking at me in the rearview mirror and smirking.

After yet another abrupt stop, our motorcade continued toward its destination. I was part of the follow car security team traveling with the president of Haiti, Jean-Bertrand Aristide. And as I was quickly learning, driving from one part of the city to another took an almost superhuman degree of cool. For one thing, if there were rules of the road, we didn't know or follow them, beyond, of course, trying not to slam into the protectee's vehicle. Without street signs, drivers navigated by landmarks, and it wasn't unusual for a road wide enough for just two vehicles to accommodate three or even four. In the city's more crowded quarters—and that was pretty much all of them—pedestrians and stray dogs made travel slow going. If we got stuck behind a brightly painted "tap tap"—an informal mode of public transportation, usually a small, multicolored truck, so named because passengers tapped on the vehicle's side to signal a stop—we had to be prepared to come to a jolting halt at any moment.

"Is that what I think it is?" I said as we slowed near an ad hoc open-air butcher's stall.

"Yup, no mistaking it: that little piggy definitely went to market."

As our vehicle passed, I got a better view of a bubblegum-pink sow's head on a wooden platter being carried through the marketplace by a man who seemed eager to sell it. My seatmate must have seen the look of incredulity on my face. He laughed.

"Not everybody's a *vegetarian*, Wilkas," he said, teasing me. It wasn't that they were selling pork or even a whole pig, it was that they were selling an oozing, freshly lopped-off pink pig's head right before my very eyes. A few feet away from the pig's head, another vendor held a few chickens by their recently slit necks, animatedly negotiating a price with potential buyers. I shifted my attention away from the market, but the view wasn't much better. No matter where I looked, there was a disturbing amount of trash. As lively as it was, Port-au-Prince was, and still is, a city in need of the most basic of services—like garbage collection.

By the time our follow car pulled in with the armored vehicle, delivering President Aristide to the site of a rally, the crowd that had gathered to greet him was already in the thousands. People were screaming, crying, holding their babies overhead in the hopes that Aristide, a former priest, would bless them. Millions of Haitians adored him, and the fervor with which they expressed this was electric. But not everyone was a fan.

The US has a long and, to put it mildly, complicated relationship with Haiti. When I arrived there, in November 1995, Aristide was about a year into his second term as Haitian president, thanks in no small part to US involvement. I use "term" lightly here, because only nine months into his initial stint as Haiti's first democratically elected president, he'd been ousted in a coup, having angered the country's rich and powerful by spearheading ambitious reforms intended to aid the nation's poor and bring to justice its bad actors. These reforms had arrived after almost thirty years of totalitarian rule, during which François "Papa Doc" Duvalier and his son, Jean-Claude "Baby Doc" Duvalier, siphoned money from already underfunded public services and created a paramilitary force to crush political opposition, the Tonton Macoute, named after the Haitian bogeyman and responsible for the deaths of more than sixty thousand people.

After he was removed from office, Aristide spent three years in exile in Venezuela and the United States. During his absence, the OAS and later the United Nations (UN) instituted trade embargos with Haiti with the intent of pressuring the military junta to back down. Instead, these embargoes exacerbated Haiti's already precarious economic and public health situations, which, combined with horrific military abuses, led thousands to flee the island.

Among those refugees were Aristide supporters who urged, via large demonstrations, the newly elected President Clinton to reinstall him. Clinton, hoping to distinguish his foreign policy from that of the Bush administration, enlisted the aid of the UN, which passed in 1994 a resolution authorizing the use of force to restore democratic leadership for a member nation—a first for the organization. Still, even with multilateral support, it wasn't like Aristide could just waltz back into the National Palace and return to business as usual. Plenty of interested parties would have liked to have seen him dead, and he had already survived several assassination attempts.

That's where I came in. Well, me, a phalanx of other US protection agents, twenty thousand US troops, and some six thousand UN security forces from twenty-four countries—a massive team effort.

About six months after I parted ways with the Darts, I received a call from a colleague who told me a guy named Jake Franklin was running a team of eleven protection agents in Haiti for the US State Department. Jake was interested in adding a female agent to the team, but finding one was proving no easy task. Female protection agents with my particular professional background and combination of skills—investigative, protective, linguistic, and travel—were, and still are, few and far between. I'm what's known as a unicorn in the industry, but unlike a mythical creature, I can be beckoned, in the right circumstances, with a mere phone call.

I was intrigued—Haiti, protection assignment, US State Department contract. Jake called me one morning from what I later understood to be the command post phone. When he explained the mission in greater detail, my ears perked up all the more: in addition to protecting President Aristide, the group I'd be working with was also responsible for training the Haitian Presidential Security Unit. Some members of the Haitian Presidential Security Unit were women, and Jake felt it would be beneficial to have a female as part of the US team. I could, he said, set a solid example for female and male Haitian agents alike.

At the end of the conversation, Jake offered me the position of "vacation guy." That's to say, I'd come on temporarily, for two months, so that a few of the other team members could rotate out on long-overdue vacations. Sure, I told him, well aware that Jake was offering me something temporary not just because there wasn't a permanent position, but because joining an eleven-man team might be an, um, interesting adjustment for everyone involved. And man, was it.

Within a week, I was in DC being briefed on the mission. I got what felt like a lifetime's worth of vaccinations—hepatitis A and B, typhoid, tetanus, and rabies—picked up a two-month supply of malaria pills, and boarded a flight to Port-au-Prince, Haiti. When we landed, I saw two guys on the tarmac wearing khaki pants, polo shirts, Banana Republic fishing vests, and hiking boots. The only way they could have been more obvious as my teammates was if they'd been jumping up and down and waving a banner that read, "Welcome to Haiti, Mary Beth."

Jake and Jim, my two new bosses, chatted with me in the car for quite a while before dropping me off at my new abode. We agreed to meet up later for dinner and they would fill in more details of the mission. The team base of operations was our command post (CP), aka Cactus, logically located within the National Palace, which was about twenty minutes from where I'd be staying. My new lodging, as Jake and Jim explained, was one of three team houses. One was called the Delmas House, after the street where it was located. The other was known as the Party House, which is pretty self-explanatory. I'd be living in what my teammates had lovingly nicknamed "the Morgue." Unlike at the two other residences, which housed four or five agents each, I'd be only the third person living in the Morgue, an apt name considering the three of us who resided there were deemed to be non-partying, boring types—obviously, we were practically dead.

As I was unpacking on my very first night in my new digs, I heard a scream from down the hallway.

"Mary! Mary!" I opened my bedroom door to see two of the house employees, Dani and Clautier. They looked scared to death.

"What's wrong?!" I said. They both pointed at the ground, where a giant tarantula was crawling toward my room. Without a second thought, I went to my closet, grabbed a running shoe, walked back out to the hallway, and heard and felt a light poof. Tarantula smushed. Mission accomplished. Welcome to Haiti, Mary Beth. This, perhaps, was an omen of what was to come.

On any given day, President Aristide would have meetings, visits, or funerals to attend in various parts of Port-au-Prince. More often than not, these missions took us to the slums: Cité Soleil, Jalousie, and Bel Air. The scale of the poverty was hard to absorb and unlike anything I'd witnessed in my previous travels. Haiti was and still is the poorest nation in the Western Hemisphere. The average home in the slums, a two- or three-room dwelling often with dirt floors, had at least six people living in it. Almost universally, the homes lacked plumbing and sanitary conditions. At the time, malnutrition and gastrointestinal diseases were responsible for more than half of all deaths. Water was unsafe, and much of the food was contaminated thanks to the lack of refrigeration and proliferation of bacteria. Haiti had one of the highest HIV infection and death rates in all of the Western Hemisphere. They also had the highest maternal and infant mortality rates. Only about one third of the population had access to health-care services. In 1996, the average life expectancy was estimated at 51.42 years, as opposed to 76 years in the United States.

On the route between the presidential palace and my humble abode, the Morgue, it was not unusual to see dozens of sick and malnourished stray dogs feasting on garbage and pigs grazing on the scraps tossed from a roadside market. People, too, would be in the streets searching for something to eat. I could have spent a hundred years in Haiti, and I don't think I would have ever gotten used to the volume of garbage strewn around the city. The first time my team, holding a protective perimeter around President Aristide as he toured a neighborhood, scaled piles of trash like they were sand dunes, I questioned my wisdom in taking the job. With few landfills and scattershot-to-nonexistent trash pickup, Haiti's poor waste management practices attracted insects and rodents and spread disease. Small wonder I'd been required to get so many vaccinations before coming into the country. How people survived the daily dangers of life in Haiti was something of a miracle to me. I later learned that, in the not too distant past, the country's largest export was human cadavers, which were sent to foreign medical facilities and studied. It was explained to me that it was a medical phenomenon that people were able to survive in such squalid conditions, and I took this as a testament of how closely connected life and death were there.

On the bright side, my team members were mostly former military types and former federal agents—for the most part, talented and solid team players. I learned a lot about these ten men during our twelve-hour shifts together: who their wives or girlfriends were, what they did in their spare time, where they hoped to be a few years down the road. Still, one of the challenges of coming on with a well-established team was that they had already bonded by the time I arrived, and seeing as they didn't expect me to stick around for more than a couple of months, no one, myself included, really put in the effort to become friends outside of work. I had my reasons for keeping my distance, but the longer I stayed in Haiti, the more bored and lonelier I got.

I was used to being the only female on an all-male protection team—that wasn't the issue here—but it felt strange and isolating to be one of the only foreign women living and working in the country. There were no female US troops assigned to the palace; in fact, if there were any female US troops in Haiti at all, they were nurses assigned to the medical unit on the nearby military base. Perhaps not surprising, there were no women among the international troops either. Within days of arriving on the job—both at the palace and in the field—I began to feel too visible, and I could tell people were curious about me in a way that could cause a world of misunderstanding if I became too friendly or familiar with them. Our conversations were strictly mission-focused for this reason, which went against my own sense of curiosity, one I'd freely and happily exercised on every one of my prior missions. After all, I loved learning about cultures and people, and the UN troops in particular comprised a hugely diverse group from around the globe.

Haiti, 1996, Protecting Haitian president René Préval

During Aristide's exile from Haiti, gangs, street crime, and vigilantism had spiked in the absence of a justice system, and the still-unstable security situation in Port-au-Prince was a major reason the UN had sent in peacekeeping forces upon Aristide's return to the capital. Wandering the streets wasn't exactly the wisest idea for a foreigner, and I felt uniquely and unusually vulnerable as a woman. There were few places I felt comfortable or safe going alone, which kept me cooped up at the command post or the Morgue more often than not. My colleagues felt confined, too, though not, as I would learn, to quite the same extent.

The minute Jake put the last letter down and sat back, I exploded. "*Furb*? *Furb* isn't a word!"

"Yes, it is!" he insisted, waving the well-worn English-Creole dictionary we kept in the command post in the air. Typical Jake.

"Oh, really? What does it mean, then?" I crossed my arms over my chest, raised my eyebrows, and waited. Jake was a world-class cheat at

Scrabble. He had hoodwinked almost every other guy on our team into believing that whatever combination of letters he put on the board was legit, but I knew better.

"It's a verb; it means 'to screw up.'" Jake dug around the velvety sack for four more wooden letters.

"That's *flub*, you jackass. Look it up."

"Furb's a synonym. Everybody says it where I'm from." In my first few weeks in Haiti, we'd already played so much Scrabble, we'd started to make up our own versions with varying rules just to keep things interesting: military-themed, proper names, foreign words, and so forth. But in none of these editions was *furb* going to fly.

"Oh, look at you—'a synonym.' Nuh-uh. Denied, Franklin."

Jake finally conceded, with a little chuckle, I claimed yet another victory, and he went off to make a phone call. We all took turns talking on the two international phone lines gifted to us by the Haitian government. One was in the command post, and the other was in our down room on the ground floor of the palace. We could make unlimited long-distance calls to the US—pretty amazing for 1995. I spent hours on the phone, depending on the week. It was my lifeline during a challenging time.

There was a single television in the command post, but there weren't that many stations, especially ones in English. CNN became a mainstay. Israeli prime minister Yitzhak Rabin had recently been assassinated, and everyone was talking about what would become of a Middle East peace plan. Also in the news: the Dayton Accords, which helped put an end to the genocidal Bosnian War after they were signed in November 1995.

Because cruising around and hanging out in Port-au-Prince solo wasn't really an option, I read more books during my months in Haiti than I have ever read in my life. Thanks to a colleague whose wife kept him supplied with Dean Koontz novels, I spent most of my evenings curled up in bed with a page-turner. I also found a random neighborhood video rental store that had a small section of movies in English. Hallelujah. Needless to say, I was a regular customer. Boring, non-partyer indeed.

Creepy crawlies notwithstanding, it didn't take long for me to realize that the Morgue was the only place I could imagine staying during my time in Haiti. The two other team houses were, to put it lightly, a little too lively for me. The Party House had earned its moniker for a reason, and what went on there wasn't my style at all. The amount of alcohol those guys consumed in a week was enough to fuel a frat house for a month. That was their outlet, their stress relief. If it had been just booze, that would have been one thing. But it wasn't.

During long days in the command post, the guys on my team would call home to their wives and kids. I often overheard these conversations, and the romantic side of me always found it sweet when they'd get mushy and sentimental with their spouse or tell a school-aged son or daughter, "Daddy will see you soon." But after hours, the family-man facade went out the window. Some of the guys would head straight from the presidential palace to the city's various red-light districts, where they would pick up a "date" for the evening. The prostitutes were mostly Haitians, though a few of the men preferred the lighter-skinned and thus pricier Dominicans who had been drawn across the border to the capital by the prospect of seemingly well-to-do American and European clients.

I was no stranger to the culture of machismo that permeated military and security circles, but the audacity of some of my teammates shocked even me. Several very married men had actually moved women into our team homes, and inevitably, when an item or money went missing, a shitstorm of accusations would follow, and the suspected concubine would be expelled from the house. A colleague I loved to work with would go on at length with me about how much he loved and missed his family, but when he finally went back to them, he left his favorite of our Haitian housemaids behind—pregnant.

It bothered me that the men treated local women as though they were disposable, but what repulsed me even more was that, in a country where adequate medical care was hard to come by and sexually transmitted infections were rampant, the men took risks with their health that could potentially impact their unwitting wives and girlfriends back home. HIV and AIDS in particular were on the upswing, not to mention the prevalence of syphilis, chlamydia, and gonorrhea. Before their R&R (rest and relaxation) rotations stateside, many of the men would seek out antibiotics and other remedies—also known as a "cleanup shot"—from one of the former Army Special Forces medics on our team.

Nowhere was the cultural divide more apparent than in my time training the Haitian protection agents Jake had told me about when he hired me. Many of them—men and women alike—were "friends" of President Aristide who had been handpicked by him to be part of his protection team, regardless of whether they had applicable skills. In 1995, the unemployment rate in Haiti was approximately 70 percent, an estimated 80 percent of the people were living in deplorable poverty, and, during much of the Duvalier regime, over two-thirds of the country's labor force did not have formal employment of any kind. Prior to Aristide's return to power, most of the people who were now protec-

tion agents had been agricultural workers, manual laborers, service workers, food-cart owners, or unemployed. Hence, many of them had come to
Port-au-Prince from the rural parts of the country.

The training was well established by the time I arrived, so before Jake
helped me take on my own trainees, I just observed my teammates instructing. Though I spoke no Creole, we had interpreters during training
and on missions; plus, some of the agents understood and spoke English.
The Haitians made a solid effort during training, which I appreciated,
given that I was as green to teaching as they were to protecting heads of
state. Still, the fact that I was a professional woman in a leadership role was
baffling to some of my trainees, as they were not accustomed to women
being in such roles.

"Emmanuel, where's Bernard?" I asked, scanning the space. Not five
minutes ago, I had assigned Bernard to his post at the recreation center
where Aristide would be speaking later that afternoon. As I did with all of
my agent trainees, I'd explained the post responsibilities and promised my
agents I would make sure they were given regularly spaced breaks. Every
thirty minutes or so, I'd rotate them with another agent at the venue.

Emmanuel followed my gaze around the room. People were starting to
filter in; my agents were supposed to have been in place, once their sectors
had been secured.

"Ah!" Emmanuel pointed toward a doorway. "He's over there, Mary,
talking to Jean-Pierre."

I walked over to Bernard and Jean-Pierre and explained to both of
them, again, what their responsibilities were and how important it was
to not leave their posts until they were officially relieved.

"Yes, Mary, yes," Bernard said, smiling gently. "We understand."

Not ten minutes later, as I made my rounds, I noticed yet another agent's post was vacant. When I inquired with a female agent, she told me he had gone to the bathroom. Scenarios I'd studied well, Rabin's assassination and Aristide's own brushes with death, flashed to mind. *If things keep going the way they're going,* I thought, *the president had better pray for good luck, if not a miracle.*

As an instructor, when your students are having difficulty learning, you question yourself. At least I do. It is an instructor's job to figure out how to get information to the students and in a way that the students grasp it. We'd started training months ago. Was our curriculum too ambitious? Were we moving too fast? Was there something our interpreters were not adequately emphasizing during class?

When I debriefed the agents after the mission, none of them thought anything had gone wrong. After all, Aristide had returned to the presidential palace just as safely as he'd arrived at the venue. When I went over what happened with Jake and the rest of the team, they just smiled. "Get used to it, Mary Beth," Jake told me. "This is how it's been since we began training and working with them. It's not their fault; they really try. All we can ask is that they do their best."

My perspective was, of course, skewed by the education I took for granted and the doors it had opened for me along the way and since. The Haitian trainees, on the other hand, lived in a country where education was compulsory for just six years—from ages six to twelve. The adult literacy rate, in 1995, was somewhere between 25 and 35 percent, which meant that between two-thirds and three-fourths of the population did not know how to read or write. Reminding myself of this didn't make it that much easier to understand how the trainees wouldn't want to take every step they could to keep their leader alive, but then again, I'd been steeped in security principles long enough that they'd almost become second nature to me. I recognized a new challenge that would take years for me to master: adopting a beginner's mindset in order to give trainees the best preparation I could. I came to realize that my role as instructor and mentor was going to require more understanding, patience, and compassion.

The house phone was ringing. And ringing. I clicked on my bedside lamp. It was a little after 1:00 a.m.

"Mary!" Clautier yelled from down the hallway. "It's for you!"

I picked up the extension. It was John, one of my teammates, calling from one of the other team houses.

"Wilkas, the presidential palace is under attack."

"What's going on?" I was instantly awake.

"I don't have time to tell you. Just get your ass in gear and get over here."

My instincts kicked in. I threw on some jeans; grabbed my gun, extra magazines, and ammunition; and flew out the door. I jumped in the car and roared down the road to John's house. Halfway there, his voice came over the radio: "Where the FUCK are you?"

"En route," I told him, taking the next curve a little faster.

When I pulled up, he was at the curb, smoking a cigarette and pacing. "Get the fuck out of the driver's seat."

I didn't argue and slid over. My adrenaline started to spike. *Oh God, oh God, oh God. What the hell are we driving into?* I thought. But I kept that to myself. All John saw was his teammate, ready and willing to head into the unknown.

If I'd floored it to get to John's, he did double-time to get to the palace. "John, can you fucking slow down? If we don't get there alive, we aren't gonna be able to help *anybody*."

When we got to the palace, John didn't wait for the gate to open. He drove right through it. The scene was chaotic, with Haitian agents running all over the place. We leaped out of the car and ran up to the command post.

Other teammates had also just arrived and were getting briefed by the two agents working night shift. Both of them had heard what sounded like shots hitting the palace and had immediately called the detail leader, Jake, who then called his shift leaders and rallied the entire team. Jake quickly put together a plan of action. We all grabbed shotguns from the weapons locker and filled our pockets with extra ammunition for our 9mm sidearms.

"Grab whatever you can hold," Jake urged, "whatever you're comfortable with. Okay, let's go."

I took a position on a balcony with another teammate with a solid vantage point of the main entry gate to the palace and the street that ran parallel to it. And there we waited. The adrenaline was ridiculous. *Cool it, Mary Beth,* I told myself. *Some of these guys are military.* Another voice popped into my head: *Who are you kidding? This is Haiti; there aren't normal rules of engagement, so get ready for a firefight.* Truth be told, I was both scared and excited. This moment is what so much of my training was about—prepare for the worst, hope for the best. I wanted there to be a firefight, I admit. I was ready.

When my heart rate slowed a bit and I got my bearings, I realized not all of my teammates had followed us out the door to take up an offensive position. As it turned out, Darryl, a colleague who loved to tout himself as the big man on campus and who enjoyed nothing more than whiling away hours in the command post bitching and complaining about how he was being treated unfairly while the rest of us pulled our weight, had taken up his own post . . . under a desk in the command post. He and another agent, Randy, had actually refused to arm themselves and join us.

On the balcony, I held my ground and peered out over Port-au-Prince. Lights twinkled in the distance, and I could see smoke from trash fires smudging the sky. Who was out there in the darkness, and what did they want? Were we dealing with a gang, disgruntled Haitian soldiers, a lone shooter?

I heard a shot, then another, but they sounded far off. We all waited and watched.

After what seemed like an eternity, Jake's voice come over the radio: "It's the prison. Stand down."

"What prison?" someone radioed back.

"The one up the road. Some prisoners tried to escape tonight. The shots were from the prison guards."

"So the palace is not the target?"

"Correct. Stand down, all."

I was kind of disappointed but breathed a huge sigh of relief and headed in. Darryl, who hardly fit under the desk, was slowly getting himself to his feet. I glowered at him, making sure he knew I had seen exactly what he had chosen to do when shit hit the fan. Then I headed to the lockers to secure my shotgun. By the time I returned, Jake was giving Darryl a stern talking-to—stern enough, I hoped, that cowardly Darryl might pack his bags and head home for good, along with Randy, who had sat in the command post smoking and chewing his nails while we all did our jobs.

Besides being too much of a pussy to do his job properly, Darryl knew, and I knew, that he had lied about his credentials. Whereas Darryl had told our teammates that he was a former Secret Service Special Agent, after about thirty seconds of talking to him when I first arrived, my bullshit meter started flashing. Sure, Darryl was from the Secret Service—the Uniformed Division.

You know the metal detector you have to go through if you show up to hear the president speak someplace? Chances are, a Uniformed Division officer set it up. Uniformed Division officers must have high school diplomas, although some have earned college degrees, and are responsible for any number of important security duties, like guarding the White House and foreign embassies in Washington, DC. Uniformed Division officers protect buildings, not people. Secret Service Special Agents, on the other hand, are an elite group of highly trained, plain-clothed professionals, who are required to have four-year college degrees. Special agents are personally responsible for protecting the president of the United States and his family, the vice president and his family, and former presidents and their families. Special agents are the first line of defense, and they're duty-bound to take a bullet for the people they've sworn to protect.

Thanks to his propensity for fluffing up his background, and for a few other reasons not worth getting into, Darryl and I didn't get along. At all. What we were doing was an honor—and also a huge responsibility: Our eleven-person team was the only group of Americans to ever protect a nation's president outside of the United States. What's more, I am, to this day, the only woman to have ever protected a foreign president outside of the United States.

Between booze and brothels, many of my other teammates were no angels, but I knew most of them would have my back in an attack. Darryl, though, was in it for Darryl—for the prestige, for the power, to be the big man on campus in a small pond called Port-au-Prince. Randy, the other guy who did nothing but give himself a bad manicure during what we thought was an attack on the palace, although a nice guy, was just a former Air Force guy who was an OK agent but afraid of his own shadow. Now that I knew what my two colleagues were capable of or, rather, what they were not capable of, I tucked that knowledge away for future use. As for my buddy Darryl, he stopped harassing me right then. No doubt he feared I would swiftly remind him of what a fucking coward he was if he even looked at me the wrong way ever again.

What had started as a two-month contract for me turned into eight months in country, during which time there was a transition in power from Jean-Bertrand Aristide to René Garcia Préval. Formerly an agronomist, Préval was the first elected head of state in Haitian history to peacefully receive power from a predecessor in office and the first elected head of state in Haitian history, since independence, to serve a full term in office. In many senses, Haiti's future seemed bright. Its present, however, was wearing me down like a grindstone. We worked twelve-hour shifts, either 7:00 a.m. to 7:00 p.m. or 7:00 p.m. to 7:00 a.m., with one day off per week.

When we traveled outside Port-au-Prince, I gained a lot of experience doing advances with next to no help, something that would be a totally foreign concept to my USSS colleagues. This was due to both a lack of functioning communications and a lack of support from the Haitians. We would often travel in a caravan of vehicles, typically just me and one other guy as the advance agents, sometimes for hours. Because there were not roadside gas stations with facilities, drinks, and so on, en route I would survey the area and find a place to pee (and poop—I know, a bit gross) in the middle of some field. Admittedly, there were times when we stopped in an area where there were some homes, and people would offer for me to use their toilet, most often a filthy hole in the ground. I would thank them and fib, saying I did not need the facilities. I preferred to risk being spied dropping my pants in the middle of a field.

When we traveled, we typically stayed in local buildings, like a school, or even outside the schoolhouse because it was so hot inside, sleeping on military cots. Showering was a rarity, and when there was a shower, it was typically a low-pressure stream of cold water. Because mosquitoes loved me, a mosquito net and coils were necessities. We often survived on MREs because the Haitians would go off on their own and rarely bring food back for us. We had a vehicle, but it wasn't like there were local restaurants, so I learned to appreciate military preparedness.

Back when Haiti had been more stable, and before its forests had been stripped for fuel during the trade embargo, it had been known as the Pearl of the Antilles. Exclusive resorts had dotted the waterfront of the Cote des Arcadins, about ninety minutes from Port-au-Prince, including the very popular Club Med. However, with the onset of the AIDS epidemic and the fall of the Duvalier dictatorship, Club Med's popularity had dwindled, and it closed in 1987. In the wake of Aristide's return and the arrival of thousands of American contractors and troops, the US government took over the former getaway as a spot to house some of its employees. And so, Club Med became, colloquially, Club Fed.

In addition to housing Americans, the place got up and running again as a low-key resort, and they began charging a daily fee for entry for those who were not housed there. You could swim, have a beer, eat a decent meal, play board games, and socialize. The rule for our team was you had to go to Club Fed with someone; you could not travel there alone. The route there took you along mostly unpaved roads, and seeing as we frequently encountered would-be thieves on the span between Port-au-Prince and the US military base, we all knew there was safety in numbers.

Club Fed was an okay option on my days off, but I didn't necessarily want to spend my downtime with my teammates, which made it less than ideal. But that inconvenience paled in comparison to something else that made going to Club Fed morbidly interesting. Not too far from where contractors drank Bud Lights and worked on their tans was a huge field known as the Boneyard. This was where the Tonton Macoute, Papa Doc Duvalier's paramilitary force, had dumped thousands of bodies. The field was a macabre testament to the Tonton's legacy of rape and murder. Scattered around the Boneyard were hundreds, if not thousands, of human bones and skulls, many with bullet holes in them. Some of the bones still had clothes attached to them. Some of those clothes were children's.

There were a few places I did venture to solo on my days off. In Port-au-Prince's rural outskirts, the roads were decent, there were far fewer people, and, most important, much less pollution and garbage. I would park on the side of the road among the corn stalks and run until I was exhausted. People thought I was crazy to go running by myself, but I carried a gun in my waist pack, had a knife clipped to my shorts, held an extendable baton in my hand, and always kept my radio with me. The few people I saw, mainly fieldworkers, would just look at me oddly as I passed. I would wave, and they would wave back. I was used to being stared at by then.

I stood out in Haiti in almost every way. I wore Western clothing, I was taller than most Haitian women by a good six inches at least, plus I was white. In a society where a caste system had long privileged light-skinned people, that created some bizarre and uncomfortable exchanges. On the rare occasions I would walk the one-and-a-half blocks from my team house to the ever-popular Star Mart to buy Pringles and Starburst, locals would either stare or reach out to touch me. So much for personal space.

One day, I dragged a French-speaking colleague along with me shopping. I went into a clothing store, where I found a few items to try on. I noticed the fitting room—there was just one—was occupied, so I stood off to the side to wait. Within moments, the saleswoman appeared, pulled back the dressing room curtain, and yanked its Haitian occupant out.

"Please, please," the saleswoman said to me in French. "You go ahead."

I was baffled, but she was insistent. When we left, my colleague clued me in: what had happened had happened only because I was white. Disturbing yet fascinating . . .

About six months into the assignment, I made up my mind that I wouldn't be renewing the current contract being offered. After two months of being the "vacation guy," I had been given a six-month extension like everyone else. When my eight months were up, I was out of there. Haiti was unlike anywhere I'd ever spent time, but the

day-to-day was getting harder to take. Despite some of their indis-
cretions, my teammates and I had maintained a professional relationship, but most of us were not good friends. Plus, I was bored,
lonely, and burned out. So much so that on April Fools' Day, my
mom and I were mid-conversation when I started slapping a ruler on
a desk. "Mom," I said, "gotta go! There's a firefight. What? I can't hear
you . . . rounds being fired."

She gasped, and I could tell I'd frightened her. "C'mon, Mom.
What's the date today?"

There was a moment of uncomfortable silence. "Mary Beth! that's
not funny." It actually wasn't, but that's what boredom can do to you,
I guess.

One day, while working at the palace, I heard shots, a fairly regular
occurrence. I immediately documented them in our command post
log, chalking it up to yet another random act of violence. Several
hours later, I was on a break and still at the command post when a
team member popped his head in to tell me I needed to come outside. I asked a teammate to take command post log duties until I got
back. We walked downstairs and made our way to one of the gates we
could not see from the command post.

There, just beyond the gate, was a shape I couldn't make out at
first. I caught the scent of gasoline, and recognized three large tires. I
realized they were around the body of a woman, and that woman was
on fire. Someone, or more likely a few people, had doused her in fuel
and decided to murder her in the most horrible way, by burning her
alive. Flames licked up her sides; it wasn't long before she collapsed
and, eventually, died. She had been accused, I learned, of being a

witch, and in a culture where Voodoo was widely practiced alongside Roman Catholicism, this kind of vigilantism was considered normal.

But it wasn't to me. I went inside and made sure this event was documented in the command post log, as I did each time something notable happened during my shift. I had a hard time sleeping that night and for many nights after. Not long before the witch burning incident, as I was driving back to the Morgue one evening, I had seen the unnaturally bent and split body of a man who'd been hacked to death by a machete on the side of the road. People walking by ignored the body, as though it was just another obstacle to be navigated on their way from one place to the next. There was not much respect for life in this place, and that, among other things, was wearing on me.

I was starting to question what I was doing with my life and beginning to notice the expertly repressed symptoms of the stress I'd been under. No matter how many miles I ran through the Haitian countryside, no distance could successfully extinguish what I felt bubbling up within me. The cognitive dissonance of trying to keep one person safe in an environment I wasn't sure would ever heal from the wounds of its history, or its present, often felt pointless. And I questioned what the hell I was really even doing in this field and with my life. I imagined some alternate universe version of my life, one where I didn't keep a go-bag by my bedside, didn't drive over stray dogs because it was impossible to avoid them without colliding with something else, didn't spend hours alone in my room because some of my teammates were off banging prostitutes.

A vision of what my life away from protection would look like was starting to take shape, and though the outline of that shape was still fuzzy, the more attention I devoted to it, the more vivid it became. Here's what it started to look like: I wanted to go back to school, spend more time with my family, live somewhere I didn't have to worry about being shot at or kidnapped or worse. I wanted my mother to sleep well, rather than wondering in the early hours of the morning whether her tough, stubborn daughter was ever going to come home.

Shortly before I gave my official notice that I wouldn't be staying on, our team accompanied President Préval to a public hospital in Cité Soleil, one of the poorest areas of Port-au-Prince. The purpose of the visit was for the president to see how pitiful the conditions were at this hospital and possibly dedicate some aid money to modernizing and staffing the place. President Préval was greeted outside the entrance by the hospital director and, accompanied by some members of the Haitian press corps, given a tour. My teammates and I struggled to stay in position as Préval moved through the building, members of the press pushing and pressing to the front for a prime position in the entourage. It was hot and humid, as it was almost every day on the island, and the crushing crowd only amplified everyone's sense of discomfort. This had happened before at other sites—the press always wanted to be the first to see and document whatever there was to see—so we were prepared. This day, however, was likely among the times they would wish they'd hung back.

The hospital director led the president down a dingy hallway to the door of what looked like a huge refrigerator. The fridge, he casually told us, was not working. He undid the latch and the door slowly moved on its large hinge. The smell that hit us was unmistakable—bodies, piled on top of each other, covered in maggots and flies. Worst of all, they were children, every last one of them. The director explained they'd died and been left in the streets. At some point, they'd been brought to this unofficial morgue, where they now continued to decompose, unclaimed. Needless to say, we lost over half of the press as they ran outside to vomit.

The Baptist Haiti Mission was about ten miles up Kenscoff Mountain from our neighborhood of Pétion-Ville. It was one of the few places that actually posted a couple of road signs guiding you there. The mission ran a network of primary schools and a hospital, trying to fill in some of the gaps decades of federal mismanagement and graft had created in education and health care. It was one of my favorite destinations, and I would escape the confines of the Morgue to visit whenever I could. The people were warm and welcoming, and they sold beautiful and delicious things in their store to support their efforts. The shelves were filled with work by local artisans: paintings, wooden chests, pottery, leather goods, Haitian vanilla, and baked goods.

During my last few days in Haiti, I sat in their teashop and considered what lay ahead for me. I wasn't completely sure, but grad school would, I hoped, give some structure to a life that, untethered from the work that had been such a big part of my identity, still seemed very nebulous and a little scary. Beside me, the huge bottles of sinfully aromatic Haitian vanilla I'd bought for my mother, all of my sisters, my friends, and myself were making my bag smell wonderful. That day I had also taken a risk, and a not inconsiderable portion of my last month's salary, to buy my mother a carved wooden chest. It would be shipped from the mission to her home, but I wasn't sure if she would like it, or if it would remind her of yet another chunk of time she'd spent worrying about my well-being.

Little did I know then that the chest would hold a place of prominence in my mother's house, and that once a year, until she died, she would spend hours sitting beside it, working oil into all the spaces she could see and all the shadows she couldn't.

CHAPTER
8

In between games of Scrabble with Jake and logging shots fired and witch burnings, I would sometimes think back, while in Port-au-Prince, to my time at the Special Agent Training Course at the James J. Rowley Training Center, outside of Washington, DC, back when I had started with the Secret Service. Whether it was shooting firearms at the various ranges, driving motorcade vehicles at the track, or taking people down in the mat room during defensive tactics, I felt like I'd found my calling. With each day and more training blocks covered, I realized that, while some of my classmates were struggling, I was calm. Everything that was being thrown at us made sense to me. For the first time, I'd really felt I was where I was meant to be professionally.

That feeling had lasted a long time, but now I missed it. I'd been prepared for ups and downs, of course, but during my months in Haiti, I'd started to feel disconnected from my work. What had once been challenging was now second nature—a good thing, on the one hand, but less than stimulating on the other. I could tolerate a lot, but between the day-to-day stress of my role, colleagues whose how-low-can-you-go standards of professionalism depressed me, and the uncertainty of waiting for the right phone call, swinging from contract to contract, hoping I'd land another interesting gig, I was pretty fried.

A big part of what I was missing, I realized, was a new challenge, a steady stream of new knowledge. And I figured out how to satisfy those desires. I decided I wanted to go back to graduate school and study forensic psychology.

One of my favorite areas of Secret Service training was in an area called Protective Intelligence Investigations. The nature of the Secret Service's protective responsibilities necessarily obligates the agency to be a proactive one. That is, while physical protection may thwart a would-be assassin, the goal is to prevent an attempt from occurring in the first place. In order to do that, the Secret Service needed to understand how people operate. The Protective Intelligence Division has a two-fold purpose: one, to evaluate the degree of danger a person, group, or activity poses to a Secret Service protectee; and two, to take steps before an incident occurs to manage that threat.

I'd pretty much inhaled any and all information coming out of the FBI's Behavioral Science Unit and pored over John Douglas's work for the FBI on threat analysis, sexual assault, serial killers, and crime classification. (You might know Douglas from the *Mindhunter* book and movies.) Understanding people and how their minds worked was one of the most interesting aspects of the job. Assessing people who might present a danger, determining what threat level they posed, establishing how often they should be monitored—it was fascinating stuff. At the time I'd thought maybe one day I'd do that kind of threat management work for the USSS, and in the years since I'd left the Secret Service, that desire had continued to entice me.

When I came back to the States from Haiti, I took a short-term apartment in downtown Chicago. My parents weren't in the area anymore, but two of my sisters were, and it felt good to be someplace like home while I found a graduate school to attend. Not to mention, going for a run was a lot easier with no gun, knife, radio, or tap taps to worry about.

After settling in, I went to the library and found a copy of the American Psychological Association's *Graduate Study in Psychology, 1996.* The section I was looking for was short. There was only one APA-accredited forensic psychology program in the entire United States, at least at the masters level, and that was at John Jay College in New York City.

I copied the contact information for the APA out of the book and headed home. It wasn't long before I had someone on the phone. I tried not to sound too desperate.

"Hi, I'm looking at the 1995 graduate study book, and I'm wondering if I have the most up-to-date version." Maybe, I thought, there was something newer. No dice. "I do? And, to confirm, John Jay College is the only APA-accredited masters-level forensic psychology program? Oh, OK. Well, thank you very much for your time." Damn.

I really, really, really did not want to go to New York City—a noisy, crowded, expensive city on the East Coast. It just didn't suit my Midwestern blood, especially when I had just started to feel comfortable in Chicago again. Besides, I was finally beginning to tame my driving after getting used to Port-Au-Prince roads. It had taken me a while to stop trying to play bumper cars on the highway, but I was reacclimating. Oh well. At least there wouldn't be tap taps in New York.

I bit the bullet and called John Jay, making an appointment to talk to the director of the program. The news I got from him was even more frustrating. He informed me that, because I had not majored in psychology as an undergraduate student, I wouldn't be admitted to the forensic psych program if I applied now. I needed six additional credits in psychology to fulfill the minimum requirements for admission. At least, he reassured me, after having asked me a few other questions, once I met the program's psychology prerequisites, I would have no problem getting in.

Completing those credits would take a little time, and I'd need some way to pay my rent and stash away some savings while I studied. A job came soon enough—but if I dreaded heading to New York for graduate school, the fact that work materialized for me in Dallas was a cosmic joke.

Few people in the US can spot a pink Cadillac without instantly thinking of Mary Kay Cosmetics. Even internationally, Mary Kay and its pink vehicles have become well-known symbols of success. While Cadillacs are only available in the US, Canada, and Mexico, a pink Mercedes Benz is the top award for the company's beauty consultants in Russia, China, the UK, and several other European countries. When I got to Dallas to become a member of the twelve-person security team protecting CEO and Chairman of the Board of Mary Kay Cosmetics John Rochon, his wife, Donna, and their three children, I was still driving my own dream car, the white, soft-top Jeep

Wrangler I'd tooled around in while protecting another wealthy family in Sarasota, the Darts. Driving around town was the first of many ways I'd learn that the Big D, as we used to call Dallas, was just not my style.

The Rochons had been the victims of an incident with a disgruntled employee, betrayed by a highly trusted member of the staff who had terrorized and aggressively assaulted one of them. Without discussing the details of the circumstances and the fallout of the incident, I can say the "disgruntled employee" was fired but never prosecuted.

Even when I was still very much in the observation and learning stages of the job, it was easy to see that the Rochons were genuinely warm, generous, and down-to-earth people. The holiday season was in full swing, and I quickly learned that the Rochons, especially Donna, were huge fans of Christmas and the whole holiday season. They had a large extended family they invited to Dallas every year to celebrate, and that meant a tremendous amount of preparation. When the week of Christmas actually arrived, all of the elaborate plans unfolded: guests touched down from various corners of the US and Canada, itineraries were distributed, parties were attended, and everyone was spoiled rotten with holiday cheer. Much of this hospitality and kindness was extended to the protection team as well.

On a day-to-day basis, my main responsibilities were to protect Donna and her daughter, Lauren, with support from two other female agents. I typically worked Monday through Friday with no set schedule. The four male agents were the ones tasked with taking Donna and John out to dinner on Friday and Saturday nights, not the females. The family thought it was more proper for a male to be driving them to dinner on weekends and that the female agents should have downtime so they could have more of a social life (read: time to find husbands). Almost every Monday, Donna would ask me how my weekend was and if I had gone out with my boyfriend. She would even ask me about the two other female agents and whether they were dating anyone.

It was the first taste I got of the Texas Southern belle mentality, and about the only aspect of it that benefited me. After all, at this point, my ultimate goal was grad school, so I took full advantage of the time off on the weekends to study. I needed it too. The truth is, though I've never been tested for it, I suspect that I might have a mild reading disorder, specifically in the realm of reading comprehension. It takes me a long time to absorb study material. So when other people are out partying or at a baseball game—or shopping for a husband—I'm reading, because it can be a challenge for me to take in what I need to. In Dallas, I made good headway with the correspondence courses I was taking to make up my missing credits, and I planned for the upcoming GREs.

Besides the Rochon family, our team of agents was also tasked with protecting the then-president of Mary Kay Cosmetics, Amy DiGeso. However, this responsibility was only during the workweek and various corporate events. Amy lived in a chic condominium in a very nice neighborhood of downtown Dallas. It was here that protection agents picked up Amy in the mornings and dropped her off at the end of her workday. The team also coordinated and worked with the uniformed security division at the Mary Kay headquarters building to establish and ensure Amy's security while in the building.

Unlike the Rochon women, Amy DiGeso was protected primarily by male agents. While it was never overtly discussed, I believe Amy specifically requested male agents. After all, she was working in a female-owned women's cosmetics company, and the majority of the employees at the headquarters building were female—that's a tidal wave of estrogen on a daily basis! Having a little male influence, a male perspective, and a splash of testosterone was probably a nice balance to her daily routine.

Still, my job often entailed interacting and coordinating with the Mary Kay headquarters uniformed security division. There was always a bit of tension between the director of their unit, Charles, and our team, mostly because Charles felt threatened by us. He felt he could manage John and Amy's security when they were in the Mary Kay building, and he did not like that we were trespassing in his territory and managing a responsibility he mistakenly felt was his. I will never forget the day I walked into the uniformed division's monthly training with our team's supervisor, Lyle. The look on Charles's face when Lyle told him that I would be the one conducting the training that day was priceless. He was speechless for a few seconds before he recovered. With an awkward smile on his face, he welcomed me and introduced me to the team, most of whom I already knew and got along with. Eventually Charles realized no one was looking to replace him and that we really did look to him and his team to coordinate John and Amy's security when on his turf. Only then did he back down and become more pleasant to work with.

Some of the women who worked at the Mary Kay headquarters were less congenial, especially at first. Without fail, every female on the protection team got nasty looks when we were seen in the building. A colleague and I were once stopped in the massive lobby by a woman with big blond hair and an elaborately made-up face.

"Excuse me, y'all?" She gritted her beautifully bleached teeth as she sized us up, her gaze lingering at our legs—or rather, our pants.

"Ma'am?" I responded, wondering what she could want.

"Y'all must be new here. Maybe you work with"—she looked us up and down again, trying hard to figure it out—"supply chain? Or . . . I'm sure I don't know. Now, you seem like nice young ladies, and I would just hate to have to say something to the higher-ups, but y'all are aware that the dress code here is mandatory? No long pants allowed?"

"Ma'am?" This time it was all I could muster.

"Skirts and dresses, ladies!" She forced her lips into a smile. "OK, y'all, I hope your day is just great!" She held the last syllable and it floated into the air and away with her.

In the field of executive protection, women agents wear a variety of attire, depending on the protectee, the event, the geographic location, and a few other factors. As an overarching rule though, we wear dress pants or a pantsuit and, with a few exceptions, a low- or no-heel shoe or boot. One of the most salient protection training principles is that, first and foremost, you have to be able to move. At any given moment. Fast. That just does not happen in skirts, dresses, and high heels. We do not work in clothes like that unless we absolutely have to in order to blend in for a special event.

That kind of incident, though, was not unusual in Dallas. The women of Dallas and I just did not get each other. I like talking to people, but I couldn't get over some of the questions I was asked. Where I come from, asking "Where do you shop?" is not a conversation starter. Especially if the only answer that wouldn't disappoint the asker was Needless Markup—oops, I mean Neiman Marcus. I knew I was doing a good job blending in with crowds while working events when, almost without fail, someone would ask me what my husband did for a living. I wish I could show you the facial expressions these women made when

I told them I was not married. I even had one or two say to me, "How old are you? You mean you are thirty-one years old and not married?" Then they'd lower their voices and say, "Are you divorced?"

Donna Rochon was a quintessential Dallas woman in some ways and, in many others, definitely was not. Sure, her hair, nails, and makeup always looked perfect, but she was also the wife of the CEO of Mary Kay Cosmetics, so that made sense. But she was originally from Canada and from a very humble family. That showed in her kind personality and in her non-showy style. Donna enjoyed nice restaurants and their country club, but she was not the type who wanted to be seen, so to speak. She would meet friends out for lunch sometimes, but she mostly kept to herself. Donna enjoyed her solitude and loved spoiling her family and spending time in the beautiful home she and John had created.

But even Donna, one day, out of the blue asked me, "Mary Beth, why don't you wear makeup?" Oh boy, did I have a lot of answers for that question. However, I chose a diplomatic one, saying, "I guess because I don't want to take the time, and I like the simplicity of it all."

"Doesn't your boyfriend like you with makeup?" she said.

I said, "My boyfriend thinks I'm pretty without it."

Conversation over.

I was out in the field with Donna when Joe, the detail leader, called me, saying he wanted me to come to his office for a meeting when I was done for the day. I didn't know what that meant. Joe and I had a good relationship, but he was a bit volatile. You never knew when he'd get angry with you, so everyone was always on their toes around him. But when I arrived at the office, Joe had a huge smile on his face.

"Mary Beth, I've got great news. You're being promoted to assistant detail leader. Actually, it's more like being the detail leader because I'm getting promoted, too, so I'll have other responsibilities."

The detail leader had the unenviable role of dealing with a lot of the bureaucracy and daily demands of the job, but, as we say in the business, "that's why he got paid the big bucks." It is a job I never wanted; I liked being a team member and then, at the end of the day, going home—without much to worry about, without the calls at all hours of the day, without being responsible for eleven other people.

"Wow, Joe. Thanks," I said, "but I think I'm going to have to decline."

"What?" Joe's jaw nearly hit the floor.

I did my best to graciously explain my position, but I could see he was starting to become upset.

"Listen. You don't have a choice here. You're taking the job."

What? I calmly said, "No. I'm not. With all due respect, you can't force me to take a position I don't want. But, again, thank you. I'm flattered." I left the office, and that was that, as far as I was concerned.

At our next team meeting, Joe spoke to the entire team: "I want to announce that Mary Beth Wilkas is the new assistant detail leader. She came kicking and screaming, but she is going to be great, and we really need her!" The team all looked at me in surprise. A few people congratulated me, but it felt more like condolences from the people who knew me better. At that point, I had about five months left on the job before I was going to be leaving for graduate school. I figured I could do just about anything for five months, even the job of assistant detail leader. Plus, after the meeting, I asked for and negotiated a nice raise. Graduate school money. Motivation.

As I suspected, there were a few changes and downsides that came with the new job title. My relationship with my teammates altered now that

I was the boss and they reported to me. When you're teammates, you're equals, and you end up having a lot of inside jokes, stories, and laughs. Now they didn't share the same stories they used to tell me as a fellow teammate, and I couldn't blame them. When there is a power difference, all of that shifts, whether consciously or subconsciously. I hated that.

I also didn't like having to deal with other peoples' problems. Donna had some issues with one of the female agents. For example, Donna asked the agent to hold her Diet Coke while she shopped. The female agent told her, "No, I need to keep my hands free."

Guess who got a call that evening from Joe, who was now the director of protective services? I was told the circumstances of what had transpired and was asked to talk with this female agent to see if she could be "a little more flexible" on the job. I understood the agent's position to a degree: a well-trained agent is focused on threats and prioritizes readiness and the protectee's safety, maybe even over her comfort. At the same time, in the private industry, that name on the right-hand side of the check is the ultimate priority, and there had been no apparent threats in the Nieman Marcus couture department that day. Unfortunately, the conversation with the agent wasn't that easy. She was letting her pride get in the way, and she was almost let go. When she understood that she was about to lose her job, she realized it was silly to not back down and be more open-minded about the day-to-day responsibilities. Disaster averted.

When we decided to hire another agent, I reviewed an impressive resume of a woman we all met and really liked. She would make a great protection agent, for sure. Even though she did not have protection experience, I could see that she was extremely bright and athletic and had major potential. When Joe and I talked with her about joining the team, we told her that she would initially be hired to work in the command post and that I would be her mentor, training her to eventually become part of the family's protection team. Now, this was a project I was excited about.

Unfortunately, my mentorship role was short-lived. About two months into her time there, when Joe called to tell me she had just been let go—as in fired—I was shocked. What the hell happened? I wanted to know. As it turned out, she had been working the night shift at the family house, and her boyfriend had shown up at the gate of the subdivision where the Rochons lived. Security from the entry gate called her and asked if she knew him, and she said she did. She not only left the command post and the house unprotected to go retrieve him, she then took him on a personal tour of the Rochon house. Are you kidding me?!

I called her and asked her about it, telling her I still thought she should consider pursuing executive protection as a career, but she told me she was too ashamed to talk to me and that she could not believe she had screwed up like that. Me either. With so few female agents in the field, we needed one as promising as her. Even now, the disappointment still stings.

The Rochons would occasionally travel to Canada, and when they did, the protection team did *not* travel with them. This was one of the few rules set by the Rochons that was not open to debate. Canada was their solace, their escape, the one and only place they could be normal people for a few days. No security, no one knowing their business. We would often plan professional trainings during that downtime. One of our teammates was actually a former instructor from the most well-known protection/defensive driving school in the world, Tony Scotti's Driving School. So, during one of those Canada trips, we had the amazing good fortune of getting the company to pay for a two-day Advanced Executive Protection driving course from a current Scotti driving instructor, and he and our teammate spent two days training us in advanced protective driving. Besides the solid skills pounded into our heads in the classroom, the actual track time was thrilling, extremely useful, and really made you rethink what you were up against in this profession. It was great to practice maneuvers on a track that I'd first learned in USSS training, like J-turns, in which a vehicle moving at high speed in reverse is quickly spun around 180 degrees and then continues moving in a forward direction of travel. It was a pure adrenaline rush and fun as hell.

The one place we were forced to wear formal dresses and high heels was Seminar, the most legendary and most looked-forward-to event of the year at Mary Kay Cosmetics. Seminar is an annual gathering of nearly thirty thousand of Mary Kay's beauty consultants at the Dallas Convention Center. The year I experienced this event, Seminar was divided into five sessions; thus, those thirty thousand consultants were divided into five groups, each named for a precious gemstone: diamond, pearl, emerald, ruby, and sapphire. Each of those groups funneled through Dallas for an unforgettable three-day production.

Mary Beth and a Mary Kay Cosmetics consultant, 1997

One of Mary Kay's mantras was "Praise people to success" and, thus, Seminar is highly focused on recognition and rewards. Although there are many levels of recognition and praise for success throughout the three-day Seminar, it is the final Awards Night where the real magic happens. In 1997, when I was at Awards Night with John and Donna, Mary Kay Ash, the company's founder, was still alive and attended each of the five Awards Night events. Wearing a long, sparkly gown, Mary Kay was walked onto center stage in her wheelchair. The giant auditorium went crazy. The roar of the crowd was deafening.

This particular year, the company gave away approximately $4 million in prizes to its top salespeople, everything from extravagant trips and diamond rings to cash and, of course, pink cars. The stage was lit up like a Las Vegas showroom. The top-selling consultants walked down a curving set of stairs escorted by admiring males, employees at the company headquarters (and jokingly called "the boy toys" by Seminar attendees). Drums rolled, cymbals crashed, and the applause was boundless, as Mary Kay herself crowned these successful beauty consultants as if they were princesses. They then paraded across the stage. It's glam, glitz, and glitter combined with praise, pride, and motivation. It's almost like a hard rock concert, only with a heck of a lot more pink all over the place. I am happy to have experienced it once, but just the thought of attending another one? Um, no thank you, one was enough for me.

Not long after Seminar, in early September 1997, I reminded Joe, the detail leader, and our team's supervisor, Lyle, that I was going to be heading to graduate school, as planned. By then, I had passed all of the courses I needed, I had taken and gotten a decent score on the GRE, and I had been accepted to the master's program in forensic psychology at John Jay College in New York City, with a start date just after the new year. I had decided that I wanted two months off before heading to school to just relax, visit family, and find a place to live in NYC. So I turned in my one-month notice to Joe and Lyle.

During that last month, Joe called me and informed me of a schedule change. Because of a scheduling issue with John's usual security agents, I'd been assigned the task of driving John to work the next morning. This was unusual, but I was glad to do it.

As we cruised from his family home to the Mary Kay building, John asked me about my academic goals and plans. Aha! Me driving John was not because of a scheduling issue but, rather, a planned event.

I told him that I'd be attending graduate school in New York soon, and he surprised me with the suggestion that I continue working with his family. I could go to graduate school in Dallas. He even encouraged me to pursue a doctorate. Then he dropped a bomb: "The company will pay for your education if you stay here in Dallas and continue working with and protecting my family."

Wow. I must have said thank you a half dozen times, and when we arrived at the headquarters building, John suggested I think about it and let him know.

Although I was very tempted by John's offer, not to mention tremendously flattered, I was ready to get the hell out of Dallas, and I needed to walk the path I had set out for myself when I left Port-au-Prince. It took me a few days to get the courage up to talk with John about my choice, but I did, and he said he understood and respected my decision. Before I left his office, he told me if I changed my mind, ever, the offer would always be there, which I thought was incredibly kind, never mind beyond generous.

I left Dallas and the Rochon family at the end of November 1997, almost exactly one year after I began the assignment. I planned to spend most of that month finding a place to live in NYC, getting to know the city, and relaxing before starting at John Jay for the winter semester in mid-January.

But that's not quite what transpired.

CHAPTER
9

NEW YORK CITY
1997

I saw thirty-three apartments before I finally settled on a place.

I was staying with my sister Peggy's college friend on the Upper East Side, in a place that was small but really nice, while I looked at apartment after apartment after apartment that tried to pass off a pantry or half of a living room partitioned by a curtain for a bedroom. It was bad enough that New York City was big, dirty, and expensive, but I'd lived in places like that before—though not on my own dime. After seeing apartments all over the city, I ended up in Manhattan Valley, not too far from Columbia University, in the first place I saw with a decent kitchen and living room and two actual bedrooms with doors that closed. Buses and ambulances went by at all hours of the day and night, but hey, at least I wasn't living in a coat closet. And I was lucky to have an awesome Puerto Rican girl for a roommate.

My mom was pretty happy. She didn't love me being in New York (though she had grown up in New Jersey and Upstate New York), but she was elated at the thought that I was getting out of the protection field. She thought I'd get my master's degree in forensic psychology and finally settle down into a normal job, have a normal life, get married, and all the rest. But even without all the rest, she was happy to have me back in the States and not in the line of fire. That was all the normalcy she really needed.

But old habits die hard. I had more than a month to kill before I started classes, and I wasn't sure I knew how to have a normal life. Plus, one more infusion of cash into my bank account before I started school wasn't a bad idea. So, when another protection job came on to my radar, I could hardly say no.

When he was murdered on July 15, 1997, Gianni Versace was just 50 years old and one of the most recognizable faces in the fashion industry. He had created a global fashion empire and was a designer to royalty such as Princess Diana and many celebrities, including Madonna and Elton John. In less than a decade, Gianni Versace had built a fashion dynasty worth over $800 million. Upon his death, Gianni Versace's brother, Santo, and his sister, Donatella, owned 30 percent and 20 percent of the company, Gianni Versace S.p.A., respectively. Suddenly, they were both in the spotlight, whereas before they had worked behind the scenes. Instant media blitz, instant recognition, instant (potential) targets. Cue protection team.

There was even more at stake for Allegra Versace, Donatella's eleven-year-old daughter. In his will, Gianni Versace had left the remaining 50 percent stake in his fashion empire to his beloved niece. The headlines across the world were quick to announce that Allegra was now worth hundreds of millions of dollars. Between her uncle's murder and the target the press had painted on Allegra's back, the family feared for her safety. Now, with the Versaces in New York for a brief stint, I was of-fered a position on the family's protection team guarding the young heiress.

When Avi, the owner of the company that had snagged the Ver-sace family security contract, called me with the assignment, my first thought was not just no, but hell no! Dallas had been a stretch. Haiti had taken its toll. But I had long told myself that I would never work the Hollywood crowd. Nor did I have any interest in being a glorified babysitter. And though in retrospect this seems like an elitist attitude, I viewed the kind of security personnel that worked these gigs with high-profile celebrity clients, many of whom wanted pro-tection as a status symbol rather than because they truly needed it, as babysitters and bodyguards. Most of the people taking such jobs had no training—at all. That big, tough guy wearing a black suit who doesn't smile? Yes, he provides a physical deterrent to a threat, but most of the time he's there to look tough and make the protectee look important. That's not how I thought of myself. My goal was not to look tough; my goal was to mitigate risk. Most often, this was done by making the protectee look less important than they were. The USSS, even the OAS ambassador in Peru, knew that. Glitz, glamour, making a show for the sake of looking important—it went against everything I knew.

I didn't say "Hell no!" on the phone, but Avi could sense my re-luctance.

"I know you're concerned about school, Mary Beth, but this is just a four-week assignment, you'll be done just before Christmas, in time for a little break before school starts. And you can stay in our corpo-rate apartment while you find a place to live for the next two years."

I hesitated, searching for a polite way to turn him down, but he jumped in before I could respond.

"Listen, why don't you at least take the day to think about it? Call me back tomorrow, OK?"

"Sure, sounds good. Thanks, Avi."

"Great. And before I let you go, let me just quickly lay out the compensation we're talking about here so you have the full picture."

It was a considerable amount. I knew having that lucrative deposit in my checking account would be most welcome for the next two years of graduate school expenses.

"OK," I said. "I'll think about it." I hung up without giving him the chance to say goodbye. Something had crossed my mind when I was talking to him. This security company was pretty well known in the private sector, particularly for protecting Hollywood A-listers, and I knew that they'd never hired a female protection agent before. Maybe it was ego, but I really liked the idea that I'd be the first one.

Of course, I knew about Gianni Versace's murder just four months earlier. Despite his wealth and fame, Gianni Versace chose to live his active and international lifestyle, day in and day out, with no known security: no driver, no bodyguard, no weapons, no home security, no training, nothing—just a belief that "it" would not happen to him. His choice was not unusual; he desperately wanted to maintain whatever anonymity he still could and live as normal a life as possible, without the burden of security. While this was a little naive, perhaps it was bold too.

And now his eleven-year-old niece had inherited all of that money. At the time, having been bequeathed an almost inconceivable sum, Allegra was graced by the press with the title of "the second most kidnappable child in the world." (Athina Onassis, the only remaining heir to her shipping-magnate grandfather, was number one on that obnoxious list.)

I made a few phone calls to colleagues who had worked for this security company and also asked around as to what the word was on the street regarding the Versace family. I didn't wait until the next day to accept the assignment. I wanted in.

I was to keep Allegra Versace Beck safe and keep the press away from her during the month she'd be in New York City. Her family wanted to make sure her photo didn't appear in the newspapers, hoping to lessen her visibility and the attention, incidents, risk, and potential for trouble that went with it.

Any ideas I had about "babysitting" Allegra went quickly by the wayside. When I took the job, I had assumed I would be working fairly short days. After all, how busy could an eleven-year-old be? I figured we would be going to toy stores, maybe see the tree at Rockefeller Center, take in the Radio City Christmas Spectacular, have a tea party or two, maybe hang out in Times Square. Allegra was a sweet, intelligent child, and that certainly made my work easier, but she also traveled all over the city, day and night.

I'd be exhausted when we finally returned to the Versace home, which was in a townhouse just off of Central Park that had belonged to Gianni. After saying goodnight to Allegra, I'd head to the command post—a repurposed coat closet on the first floor that doubled as a down room. After checking in, I'd ask where Ray, Donatella's protection agent, was, so we could coordinate for the next day. Almost every night, the command post agents would tell me, "Oh, he went home hours ago." Although Donatella was quite socially active, many of her evenings ended with groups of friends at home, which meant Ray's work was done once she was in for the night.

Allegra had lunch with friends, went to dinner and the theater with her father, browsed at high-end stores with a personal shopper, met for "play dates" with various famous people's children, and spent afternoons with huge celebrities. She also spent quite a bit of time during the first week of December with her mother at the Metropolitan Museum of Art, but not on a schoolgirl's gallery visit. Each year, the Met holds a formal Gala, which benefits the Met's Costume Institute, and each year's event celebrates a specific theme. In 1997, that theme was Gianni Versace. Donatella spent most of her time that week at the Met getting the exhibit ready for the Gala on December 8, and Allegra was right there beside her. From the Met, it wouldn't be uncommon for us to hop in a waiting car and head across town for a play date.

On one such ride, to visit one of her friends in Manhattan, the son of a famous sculptor, Allegra asked me from the back seat of the car if we could open her window. I looked at the driver and gave him a nod, a signal to roll the window down from his control panel since he had the child locks on.

"Sure, hon, no problem. But just a little, OK?" I didn't want her face exposed to the busy street.

"Mary Beth?" she replied, in her very pronounced, but delicate British accent. "Why do you always say 'hon'?"

Shit. I could see the driver quietly chuckle as I grimaced and rubbed my face in my hands, cringing. I realized I had been calling Allegra "hon" and "sweetie" more and more since the assignment had begun. Somewhere along the way, it had just begun to slip out.

"I'm sorry, Allegra, it's just habit. I'll stop," I said. I was horrified that I'd address a protectee like that. It was not appropriate.

She then said, "Well, I don't really mind, I just wanted to ask you why you always say that." Needless to say, I was very cognizant of how I addressed Allegra from that point forward.

Sometime around mid-December, when I reported to the command post at the Versace house, I was told Donatella's assistant wanted to speak with me. I had already learned a lot about the various personalities of this protection detail, including most of the Versace staff. Donatella's assistant at the house was not going to lower himself and come to talk with me; rather, he wanted me to come and find him. I found him in the kitchen and, while he continued to eat his breakfast, he informed me that Allegra would be spending the day with Sting and Trudie Styler's seven-year-old daughter, Coco. He explained that I would take Allegra to their house in the city, pick up Coco and her nanny, have lunch, and head over to FAO Schwarz to do some Christmas shopping.

I admit, I was excited at the prospect of possibly meeting Sting; after all, the first band I ever saw in concert was the Police, when I was sixteen. Sting and Trudie Styler lived in a very nice building on Central Park West in Manhattan. It was one of those buildings where, once the doorman clears you to go up, he directs you to the elevator where he has already remotely pressed the appropriate floor number. What I did not expect was that, once the elevator stopped, the door would open right into the family home. In other words, it's not like we walked off the elevator and had to find the appropriate apartment number; they had the entire floor, two in fact. It instantly made sense to me, then, why the doorman was the one controlling the elevator.

Trudie Styler greeted us and told Allegra that Coco was in her room waiting for her. I waited next to the elevator. Trudie Styler was striking in appearance and had a very kind and humble presence. A few minutes later, the elevator door opened, and Sting walked out, brushing my right shoulder. He said, "Oh, excuse me," and then hello. I returned the greeting and, because he looked at me with a puzzled look, I told him I was with Allegra Versace. He said, "Oh. That's nice," and disappeared into the house. I have to admit, it was the highlight of the month-long job for me.

A few minutes later, Coco's nanny came down the hall and introduced herself. I liked her instantly. She was laid back, spunky, and sarcastic. On the drive to the famous toy store after lunch, I let the nanny know we were expected in a few minutes at the back door of the store. She asked what I meant by "expected," and I said, "Oh, I'm sorry, we have an appointment. An FAO Schwarz personal shopper has been arranged for Allegra, and she will meet us at the back door in a few minutes." The nanny was not fazed at all; this was the world she was used to operating in, but it was all new to me.

Sure enough, a few minutes later, we rang the bell of the back door and were greeted with a big smile. I had no idea what having a personal shopper was going to entail. I just continued to do my job, protecting Allegra, while observing this fascinating setup. While walking through FAO Schwarz, I received a call from Ray. He was passing along a message from Donatella asking me to make sure we purchased a Christmas gift for Coco and Giacomo, Coco's two-year-old brother.

I asked Coco's nanny if she knew what her charge wanted for Christmas.

"Well," she said, "this morning Coco said that she wanted a penis!"

"Uh . . . I don't think we'll find one of those here." We both laughed.

I let Allegra know the plan, and she aptly picked out great gifts for both kids. Allegra knew exactly how all of this worked; she was a pro. She never asked for guidance and never even looked in the direction of the personal shopper. All she had to do, while walking through the store, was point to something and the personal shopper would mark it on her clipboard. It was all very subtle—no eye contact was even made. To be honest, I was mesmerized. And it all magically made its way to the Versace home, beautifully wrapped and ready to gift. Allegra was no average child.

One morning Ray greeted me in the command post and told me that we'd be going with our protectees to visit Madonna and her baby, Lourdes. After a short visit, which involved lavishing the child with gifts, Donatella and Ray left. Allegra, however, chose to stay longer to ogle Lourdes and chat with Madonna. Eventually, Madonna announced that they were going to be walking to Rosie O'Donnell's place several blocks away. I offered the car and driver we had waiting outside, but Madonna said she wanted to walk.

From the minute Allegra and Madonna left the building, they were surrounded by fans and paparazzi. They started to chase our group, snapping photos and shouting out questions. "Madonna, your baby is so beautiful!" someone called out in a heavy Italian accent. A husband-and-wife couple wielding cameras was trying to keep pace with us on their bicycles. As they swerved off into the crowd, the woman called out, "Oh my god, Madonna, you are so beautiful! Pose for the camera, Madonna. Please, Madonna!"

Now, as good security protocol dictated, our security driver was shadowing us the entire time, meaning he was moving slowly down the street in the vehicle, parallel to us. If there was any type of incident, the vehicle would be close by for me to evacuate my protectee.

Annoyed by the people following us, I appealed to Madonna again. "Why don't we take our car and drive to our next stop so we can avoid this? I don't want to put Allegra at risk."

Without even looking at me, she blurted out, "Fuck 'em. They're all vultures and assholes anyway."

I hid my annoyance, and just said, "OK. But it would be best to get in the car and drive over to Rosie O'Donnell's home. I'd like to get Allegra away from the cameras."

She looked at me like I was crazy, but only briefly, before marching on without even pausing to consider getting in the vehicle.

Maybe she just wanted to prove that she could "live a normal life" and walk the streets of New York City as if those fans and paparazzi did not exist. Maybe she was used to the crazy level of attention and had come to expect it whenever she left her home. However, knowing she was walking with a minor who was a celebrity herself, and considering what had happened to Allegra's uncle, it seemed to me that Madonna should have known better. Madonna was one of Gianni Versace's close friends, and Allegra was the golden child—it was too perfect a story for any tabloid to pass up.

I turned to Allegra and said, "I'm sorry," as I grabbed the whopping bag of gifts she was carrying for Rosie O'Donnell's kids, Chelsea and Parker. "I'm going to need this."

I held the bag in front of Allegra in an attempt to shield her face from the cameras for the whole walk. By the time we arrived at

Rosie O'Donnell's building, the crowd had, thankfully, left us alone. They'd gotten what they wanted, I guess.

We entered the reception area where there were two doormen. One of the doormen greeted them, asking whom they were there to visit. Madonna responded, "We're here to see Rosie O'Donnell. She's expecting us." Now, here is the best part of the story. The doorman then says to Madonna, "And you are?" The look on Madonna's face was priceless—a combination of disgust and incredulity—as she spit out, "Ma-don-na." Then, the other doorman said, "Dude, I cannot believe you asked that!" I wanted to high-five the guy but kept my reaction to a smirk as we were given the go-ahead to head up. You could still hear the chuckles as the elevator door closed.

Rosie was outside of her apartment waiting for us. The smiles on their faces reflected two longtime girlfriends who were really excited to see each other. Rosie, with her New York accent, said, "Hi, Mo," and Madonna responded, "Hi, Ro." Then Rosie said, "And you must be little Allegra. You are so cute. Come on in." Allegra, with her sweet British accent, smiled and told Rosie it was nice to meet her. As Madonna and Allegra walked into Rosie's apartment, I stayed down the hall near the elevator, with the intention of standing outside Rosie's door once they were inside. Rosie O'Donnell then turned to me and said, "And you must be the security person. Why don't you come in, security person?"

I said, "Thank you, but I'm fine out here."

In her quintessential Rosie way, she said, "You security people, you always think you have to suffer. And why don't you ever smile?

Just come in, sit down, and have a glass of water or something."

As I was about to refuse, yet again, Allegra said, "Come on, Mary Beth, please come in. I want you to come in."

OK. OK. OK. I walked in and Rosie said, "See, security person, isn't this much better!" She laughed and then introduced herself, and I did the same.

Although I knew I was better placed outside Rosie O'Donnell's apartment door, I opted to sit inside with a view of the door for a few reasons. For one, this was an unplanned stop, so no one knew that Allegra was here. Had the press followed us all the way to Rosie's building, word might have gotten out about Allegra's whereabouts, and then I might have stood my ground outside the door. However, because no outsiders knew Allegra was here, except the doormen, any kind of a coordinated attack or kidnapping was highly unlikely. But this was also a bit of a tricky call for any agent in this position to make. Normally, when you are placed outside an entryway, you have access to the interior area so that you can get to your protectee if you need to. Either the door is open or, say, in the case of a hotel room, you have a key. I did not have a key to Rosie O'Donnell's apartment, and I was not going to ask her for one. In the end, I thought Allegra was best served with me inside and close to the door even though standard protocol would have me outside it.

Not surprisingly, a photo of Allegra with Madonna was, in fact, published in a New York City newspaper the next morning. Needless to say, all hell broke loose. When I walked into the command post the next morning with Ray right behind me, our boss, the owner of the security company, was already there. He had not let us know he was coming. Ugh.

Each of us was interviewed individually—me, the driver of Allegra's vehicle, and the command post agent on duty at the time. Even Ray was grilled, despite that fact that he had left Madonna's place with Donatella well before the incident happened. Thankfully, all of our stories matched, and it was clear there were several attempts to avoid the incident. When I shared the part about taking Allegra's shopping bag from her and holding it up in front of her face, the owner of the security company laughed. I asked what was so funny, and he said that the shopping bag, along with my arm holding it, had made it into the photo and, until that moment, he had been wondering what it was. In the end, we were all told, if not ordered, to continue to do our best to avoid having Allegra's photo in the papers.

Christmas was coming up soon, and there was a day of holiday fun planned for Allegra. I had arrived early to the Versace house one morning, expecting things to be very quiet, as they typically were until about 11:00 a.m. or so. Instead, I walked into a house full of frenetic energy. I stepped into the command post and asked what all the activity was about and was told, "Oh, thank god you got here early! All activities have been cancelled for Allegra and Donatella today. You and Ray will be heading out in a few minutes. Get ready to move ASAP." Ray had entered the house about a minute behind me, so we were ready to go. I looked at Ray, and we both just shrugged, not having a clue as to what was going on. Nobody was sharing, either.

Next thing I knew, we were speeding up the West Side Highway. About fifteen minutes later, our motorcade came to an abrupt halt at a large hospital. I still had no idea what the heck was going on, and neither did Ray; no one said a word in the vehicles the entire trip, and the tension was palpable. We simply followed everyone into the hospital. Although no one talked to me specifically, it was clear they were doing a series of tests and evaluating Allegra. A few minutes later, I heard a doctor say, "Mrs. Versace, we have to get your daughter to the cardiac unit. Now!" I was stunned. She was eleven years old! What could possibly be wrong with her heart?

The group rushed from one medical unit to the next. I could tell they were not trying to figure out whether this was a common cold or the flu. Amid the chatter, I overheard the terms "anorexia nervosa" and "eating disorder." The look on Donatella's face was painful; she was in such a vulnerable position, and she was clearly terrified for her daughter. It was scary to me, and I barely had a sliver of the full picture yet. Now that I have a lot more knowledge on eating disorders, I understand the potential damage anorexia can do to the heart, along with the brain, kidneys, hormones, muscles, and other parts of the body.

For a long time, I didn't discuss this incident or Allegra's health with anyone outside of the Versace family's protection team. Security agents, whether protecting the president of the United States, a foreign dignitary, or a fashion icon, hear a lot of information that is not their business to repeat. A protectee needs to know that their private lives are just that— private. But in 2007, ten years after her diagnosis, Allegra's parents issued a public statement about their daughter's battle with the illness. Since then, I've made a choice to be honest about the scope of my experience with the family, which, unfortunately, included helping the family and the team keep Allegra safe in the midst of a health crisis.

The Versace family left New York to spend Christmas on a beautiful Caribbean island; I was tasked with doing the advance at the airport.

That meant going to Teterboro in New Jersey a couple of hours ahead of the scheduled departure time, ensuring the pilots were, in fact, who they said they were and that they were getting the plane ready for the trip, overseeing the loading of the family's luggage, making sure all packages had arrived and were on board, and sweeping the plane.

Sweeping the plane means to clear it, like you would clear a room for explosives or anything else that does not belong there that could cause the clients harm. Essentially, I was responsible for making sure the Versace family was flying on a plane that no one had tampered with. Being the advance agent at Teterboro also meant I made sure all the appropriate people at Teterboro were in place when the Versace family arrived in their small motorcade, that gates were opened at the appropriate times, and there was no press, paparazzi, and/or fans in the vicinity. Finally, my advance duties entailed being the point person for the family once they arrived at the airport. The drivers looked for me and made sure I was standing where I was supposed to be—at the bottom of the private plane's staircase. This was our subtle signal that everything was cleared and ready for the family to board. Had I not been there or had I been standing at a different part of the plane, that would have signaled that something was wrong and for the vehicles to leave the area immediately.

As the family vehicles entered the airport and were making their way toward me, a window rolled down, and I heard Allegra scream, "Mary Beth. Hi, Mary Beth." I had to laugh. Before the car was parked, she had the door opened and was running toward me. She hugged me and gave me the wrapped box in her hand and said, "Thank you, Mary Beth, and Merry Christmas!" I barely got out the words "Thank you and Merry Christmas" before she had disappeared up the stairs and onto the plane.

Allegra's parents checked her into a specialized inpatient eating disorders program. I was asked to work one of two twelve-hour shifts at the center where the program was housed and to be part of her long-term protection detail in the United States.

I surprised myself by feeling tempted. I had unwittingly become attached, or maybe just very protective, of Allegra. But how long could I stand in a hallway guarding someone on the other side of a door during an intense treatment program? I knew the answer to that: as long as it took. I could protect her. Most likely, nothing would happen. Maybe I'd save her one day— from some threat, a kidnapper, an incompetent bodyguard, an unscrupulous friend. Maybe from herself.

But I wouldn't be happy doing that.

I thought back to the USSS—not to my training, but to the feeling of losing my job, of being told that I wouldn't be an agent anymore. And I thought back to Spain, after losing my shot with the FBI. I thought of Marlin Johnson and of my dad saying—not telling, but believing—that I'd be a Charlie's Angel, that I'd be whatever I wanted to be.

What did I want to be? I knew the answer now, I thought. I wanted to be a person who helped women, including young girls like Allegra, who needed it. But the way for me to do that wasn't by guarding doors, nor would I focus on eating disorders. It would be by completing the master's program in forensic psychology at John Jay College, and by combining the education I gained with the experiences and knowledge I had from a career in protection.

In the years that followed, I did just that. I worked as a counselor in the stalking unit within victim services in Queens Criminal Court, and I've researched and written about stalking—creating a stalking risk assessment prototype, coauthoring a chapter of a book on stalking trauma syndrome, and providing anti-stalking training and seminars around the country. I was doing what I set out to do.

In 2000, John Rochon, who, true to his word, had been hugely supportive of my pursuit of graduate education, insisted that I speak at the legendary Mary Kay Seminar. The Mary Kay Ash Foundation was expanding its mission from cancers that affect women to also include violence against women. I had only recently graduated, and I was uncomfortable, at first, in my role as an expert on such an important subject. I also wasn't very comfortable with the many women who came up to me after the talks, some crying, all thanking me for my talk and telling me how helpful it was. I was far more comfortable being in my usual role of protector, which kept me in the shadows. But eventually I realized that regardless of how uncomfortable I might have been speaking in public, I had something to say that people, especially women, needed to hear. I'll always be grateful to John for pushing me to speak at the seminar. The experience, I'd realize later, played a crucial role in growing my confidence as an instructor and trainer.

As my career moved further in this new direction, it seemed like my work in protection was over, part of my past. But that turned out not to be the case. I'd become involved in protection again in ways that surprised me.

CHAPTER
10

"Thank you, Wayne," the deputy district attorney from the San Diego DA's office said from her seat at the head of the table in a crowded conference room in the downtown San Diego Hall of Justice. The lead investigator from the DA's office had just finished presenting the details of a stalking case. "And now, I want to open up the floor for your thoughts."

A middle-aged man in the front row raised his hand and wagged his index finger.

"Please, go ahead," said the woman from the DA's office, nodding at him.

"The first thing we really need to consider, it seems to me, is . . ." The forensic psychologist had a slow, deliberate way of speaking. "How can we be sure there's no malingering involved here?"

The victim advocate sitting next to me shifted in her chair, uncomfortable at the suggestion as the psychologist laid out his case.

"From what we've heard so far . . ."

I took notes and began to prepare my own questions before weighing in. I would want to know more about the history of the perpetrator and the victim. Looking around the room, I could see the other experts and stakeholders in the room—law enforcement, mental health, victim services, legal professionals, and more—all eager to jump in with their own thoughts, opinions, and suggestions for how to proceed.

I was a member of the San Diego County District Attorney's Office's prestigious Stalking Case Assessment Team, a multidisciplinary special unit organized to address issues of victim safety and threat assessment related to stalking. We'd listen to presentations on active stalking cases and give our recommendations on how the agencies involved should proceed. It complemented the writing I'd been doing on stalking and stalking-related trauma, as well as the speaking gigs I'd begun getting on the topic of violence against women. I was really happy, doing fascinating, rewarding work, and living in a city I loved. I'd wanted to live in San Diego for a long time, and it was everything I'd dreamed of.

So, when I got a call about a job from Tom, who I'd worked with in Haiti, I wasn't too enthusiastic. It was 2001, in the middle of the summer, and I'd just returned from a run on a beautiful, sunny beach—which wasn't helping his case at all.

Tom told me he was putting together a team of instructors for a course in VIP Protection for the State Department's Antiterrorism Assistance (ATA) program, and he wanted me on board. It was a pilot program, so he promised the initial commitment would only be for three weeks in the fall.

I was, however, reluctant to dip my feet back into the field, even briefly. I really wanted to leave the past in the past and move forward with my new career path. On the other hand, I told myself, I already had a trip planned to Colorado the following month, so what could it hurt to add a stop in Albuquerque for two days to check things out?

Mary Beth instructing during "Save the VIP" training, 2004

When I visited the ATA academy in Albuquerque, I was impressed with the whole operation. The ATA had existed since 1983, and now it was expanding. The program needed a place to house a variety of courses outside of the central office of the US State Department in Washington, DC. Albuquerque was chosen as the central training location, with two other smaller facilities in Socorro, New Mexico, and Baton Rouge, Louisiana, where specialty courses were taught. The program had rented a very nice building for classrooms and administrative offices. In addition, they had made arrangements to utilize some of the shooting ranges at Kirkland Air Force Base, as well as several acres in a remote area of the base for practical exercises. About thirty minutes from the main building location was Sandia Speedway, where the program would eventually conduct driver and motorcade operations training. It was hard to resist such an impressive and well-organized program. Plus, I was instantly addicted to New Mexico's famous green chili. By the time I left, I had been formally offered a three-week contract as an instructor for the course slated for early October, just a couple of months away.

Then 9/11 happened.

Like so many others, in the aftermath of the tragedy in New York, I felt a pull to do my patriotic duty and help in any way I could, especially since I had only left the city two years earlier. With my background in mental health, I hoped I could help the survivors and families of victims. I called the Red Cross first, and I learned they had been inundated with offers for help and were in no need of more volunteers. That was great for them but disappointing for me. They thanked me and gave me the names and contact information of several other organizations to reach out to. I called each of them and heard the same response—they all had an abundance of volunteers and did not need my help.

I believe things happen for a reason, and this was no exception. If they didn't need me in NYC as a volunteer, I figured, all the more reason to head to Albuquerque and serve the country in a different way.

The mission of the ATA VIP Protection program was to train friendly foreign nationals—generally high-level law enforcement and military operators—in the art of executive protection. The first students—a delegation from Bangladesh—were due to start their training in October, and as I continued my work in San Diego, I began to wonder if the program would be put on hold, like so many things were in the aftermath of the devastating terror attacks.

I called Tom to confirm that we were still on.

"I mean, considering what had just happened," I started, "is the State Department really focused right now on assisting other countries with their terrorism problems? Particularly one so close to where we believe those responsible for 9/11 are from?"

Besides being head of our team, Tom was a former State Department Diplomatic Security Special Agent, so I thought he'd know more about what was going on.

"It's funny," he answered. "I actually had the same question. You know what they told me?" I heard the emotion in his voice, a mixture of pride, excitement, and urgency, as he continued. "They said abso-fucking-lutely. This makes them want to do it even more. We're training these guys to fight terrorism. We're going to bring them in, and, who knows, maybe them, maybe the next class, maybe somebody can help stop something like this from happening next time. Here, in Bangladesh, wherever. We gotta fucking do this, Mary Beth. Are you still in?"

I didn't need a speech. I was in.

If it hadn't been for the experiences I'd had in grad school, in psychology, and in public speaking over the previous years, I'm not sure how I would have handled myself in front of a classroom of students at the ATA. Even so, I was excited but a little insecure about teaching my first class. I spent days practicing how I'd present the material, going over the PowerPoint slides, deciding how I would emphasize a point, predicting what questions might come up, and anticipating a dozen other potential scenarios.

In fact, I had a few questions of my own about some of the material.

Before I'd arrived, Tom and two of the other instructors, Wayne and Dave, had updated and rewritten much of the VIP Protection course curriculum. Most of the new ATA training material I was reviewing lined up with my training and experience, but I'd noticed a few differences—nothing that was wrong, per se, just information that was not exactly synced up with what I knew. For example, our ATA curriculum might call for the term *follow car* versus *follow-up car*—minor things like that.

At one of our meetings before the first class, I brought it up. All five instructors were sitting around the table at the Persian restaurant that had quickly become our lunchtime hangout.

Wayne, who was a retired US Secret Service Agent, smiled and slapped the table. "Ah ha! I told you!" he shouted at Dave, who groaned in response.

"Oh gawwwwd, give me a fucking break, Wayne. Plus, this is a State Department program, and you two need to get with our lingo." Dave was from Georgia, and his accent was thick. Like Tom, Dave was a former US State Department Diplomatic Security Agent, though he had been running his own successful investigative company for the past decade. It turned out that the different factions had argued about some of these things while they were updating the course materials. The differences I'd noticed had been debated, and the State Department side had won out.

Wayne looked at me and said, loud enough for the whole table to hear, "Let's let it slide, Mary Beth. You know, we protect the president and vice president of our country. State Department agents don't have the clearance to know any more than that." I laughed and saw Tom turn red as he bit into his kebab. Dave just rolled his eyes, cleared his throat, and said, "Again, this is a State Department program, and you two are just fucking lucky to even be here." We all laughed out loud.

That was the beginning of the banter that lasted for the entirety of our time together, with me and Wayne on one side, and the State boys, Tom, Dave, and Eli—who had worked at the US Embassy in Lebanon with Tom—on the other. They definitely got their jabs in as well, but, of course, they were pretty weak. It was just one aspect of the phenomenal dynamic that the five of us developed both outside of the classroom and in it.

An often-unseen dynamic exists within a close-knit team of security professionals. This dynamic involves the mechanism by which psychological bonding and friendship happens. This bonding is important and necessary for a tight team to function in high-stress environments. It is affectionally called "giving each other shit." Regardless of race, sex, or religion, the banter and back-and-forth of day-to-day work centers around comments, jokes, and ribbing about what, by normal societal standards, would be off-limits or very sensitive. Yes, these kinds of comments are often sexist or politically incorrect, but they are important to building this unique bond. In normal, everyday life this does not occur. You cannot "give each other shit" in an office or community environment, but in my experience, among my colleagues, it is not only acceptable, but a welcomed and necessary part of building the bond among a team. It means you have to develop thick skin and see the bonding banter for what it is. My relationship with Dave developed into a great friendship because we gave each other so much shit—every day.

"Did June take your last name when you guys got married?" I asked him one day.

Dave did a spit take and started laughing so hard he could barely respond. "Are you fucking kidding me? I mean, look at me. Of course she did!"

Truth be told, I was really annoyed by Dave's response. So, I immediately went down the hall, found Eli, and asked him if his wife took *his* last name when they got married. Eli clearly sensed something was brewing as Dave was shouting down the hall, "Don't be a suck up, Eli."

Eli smiled and calmly responded, "Well, she did, but I would have respected her decision had she chosen to keep her own name." Dave rolled his eyes, let out a "Pleeeaassseeeee," and told Eli he was a traitor.

During the three weeks that each foreign delegation was in Albuquerque attending the VIP Protection course, there was always one official night when we went out to dinner together with the students. This tradition began with our first class from Bangladesh. Toward the end of this dinner, Dave came over to the table I was sitting at. We happened to be talking about the customs surrounding marriage in Bangladesh. Dave, being Dave, although I barely knew him at the time, decided to spice up the conversation and began asking the delegates if they were married and how the tradition worked. For example, did a Bangladeshi man need his future father-in-law's permission? One of the younger students smiled and said that, yes, he had to get permission, plus he had to give the father-in-law a sizable dowry for the daughter.

Dave feigned surprise and told them that, in America, the father of the bride paid the young man to take a daughter off of his hands. I burst out laughing. Of course, Dave did not say that this was in the form of paying for the wedding; no, he let them think that American men were so special they received money when they married. The Bangladeshis let out a collective howl of surprise.

Dave edged closer to the group and said, "Colonel, you're not married. What do you think of Mary Beth? She's puurrrrdy, isn't she?"

The colonel nodded, not at all embarrassed. I wanted to tell Dave to shut the fuck up; however, that would not have been appropriate given the company. I honestly could not believe this conversation was even taking place. Thankfully, I rarely blush, or my face would have been bright red.

Dave did not stop there. Nope. He looked at the entire table, acting all authoritative, and said, "Well, how much . . . how much would you pay for Mary Beth? As the senior man in this room I can negotiate a price for her, right here, right now!"

WHAT?! At this point, I could have either stuck a fork in the side of Dave's neck or sat back and enjoyed the entertainment. I chose the latter. Oh, don't misunderstand me, I was mortified, but I was partially enjoying watching the speeding train and interested to see how Dave was going to handle the carnage. From me and the students.

One student shouted, "I give six cows!"

Dave yelled, "Six cows, dayyyuuummm. The other student gave five for his wife." He then got even closer to the group and whispered, as if I couldn't hear, "Guys, that's insulting. Do you want to insult Mary Beth?" With his audience captivated, Dave said, "No! I didn't think so!"

Dave then used his hand to show me off, like a gameshow host would a car on the studio floor, just waiting to be won. "We all agree Mary Beth is pretty, right?"

"YES!" they nearly shouted.

"OK, now look at her, she's pretty, in good shape, smart. She's a little skinny, but don't worry about that, she'll fatten up once you get her back home."

You can't make this shit up, I thought.

Dave continued, "Her hips are a bit thin, but as long as it ain't trip-lets, she'll probably push out three sons for you real fast!"

"I give twenty cows!" a student proposed.

"Twenty?" Dave shouted. He stood up and, again, used his hand to display the merchandise—me. "You're only gonna give twenty for this?! Mary Beth and her family are going to be horribly insulted."

Hands shot up and offers were tossed out like we were at an art auction, "Fifty!" "One hundred!" "One hundred seventy-five!" The excitement was palpable.

Then the colonel, who had remained silent since his nod of acknowledgement, pounded his fist on the table and said, "Five hundred COWS!" He was the class leader and ranking officer of the whole group. The room went silent, and the offers ceased.

"Now, that's more like it!" Dave laughed. "OK, now I have to talk with Mary Beth and her father to convey the offer. I think this is very fair, but her father will have the final word."

Dave then grabbed me by the arm and led me from the room. He was laughing so hard, he had to take off his glasses to wipe the tears.

"Dave!" I shouted at him. "Are you fucking nuts? You just fucking sold me to the Bangladeshis! Are you flipping kidding me? This is crazy, embarrassing, and just plain wrong!"

Trust me when I tell you this did not even faze Dave. He was too busy laughing, telling me not to worry because he would tell the colonel that my father was not ready to let go of his precious daughter. "No, Dave. You can tell him you are an asshole and that I have a boyfriend. This is insane!"

After about ten minutes, Dave walked back in to see the colonel, who was undoubtedly talking to the group about what was going to happen on our wedding night. "Colonel. Please do not be too disappointed, but Mary Beth's father feels the offer is just too low. Also, he will not allow his daughter to live in a country so far away. He thanks you for your interest though."

"But that's all I have, Dave, and Bangladesh is a wonderful country. Mary Beth will be very happy there."

"I know, I know, Colonel. Who knows, you are here for two more weeks. Maybe another beautiful American girl might be available."

On the day the Bangladeshi delegation left from the Albuquerque airport, we were there to see them off. As he headed to airport security, the colonel looked at me and said, "Miss Mary, the offer still stands if your father changes his mind."

I just nodded, waved, and waited for him to pass through security before I punched Dave in the arm. Once again, he was laughing so hard he could hardly walk.

To this day, every time Dave and I get together, he finds someone to tell that story to, and every time the truth gets a bit more exaggerated.

When the first VIP Protection course began, I was responsible for training on topics like walking formations and motorcade operations. Then we went over and analyzed a real scenario, the attempted assassination of President Ronald Reagan. Wayne had actually been working in the second ring of security for the president that day, so he had plenty to share. When I taught concentric rings of security, I asked Wayne if he would co-teach with me and, without hesitation, his response was, "Of course."

We had to improvise some with the group from Bangladesh. Many of the students were high-ranking officers and, as such, for many years had their own chauffeurs. As a result, their driving skills had understandably depreciated—as in they didn't remember how to drive. So Dave and I were chosen to spend some extra hours with a few of them after class re-teaching them the fundamentals of driving. Teaching basic driving skills was not the most fun part of that course, but seeing the faces of those same students after they executed a J-turn on the track in week three was priceless.

When the three weeks of class were complete, we held a formal graduation ceremony. Mike Harris, who was the ATA regional manager from Washington, DC, and based in Albuquerque, spoke at the graduation ceremony. Mike was a former Secret Service agent, and he was a hard-charging man with boundless energy, a great family, and a can-do attitude. He'd observed much of the instruction first-hand and surprised us when he spoke about our performance as trainers, describing how hard we worked, how well we interacted with and treated each delegation, and our camaraderie. The words he used have stuck with me to this day, and I often use them myself in his honor: "Perfectly perfect." With a review like that, it was no surprise that the State Department gave the VIP Protection course the green light to continue. Tom, Wayne, Dave, Eli, and myself—we referred to ourselves as the Fantastic Five—would continue teaching as a group for over a year.

Our second class was a delegation from Kazakhstan. They were a stoic and fascinating group, who didn't fully trust the Americans they were learning from—there seemed to be some lingering suspicion from the Cold War.

One day after driver training, we were debriefing in an auditorium—Tom, Eli, Dave, Wayne, and I were sitting up on the stage, and the students were in the seats below. Eli had fielded a question from the students and had explained some training based on US State Department operational procedures. The back-and-forth continued.

"So that's how we deal with that. How does that compare to your experience? How would you handle the same situation in Kazakhstan?"

Without skipping a beat, one of the students responded in commanding Slavic tones. The female translator told us what he'd said while the students sat stock still: "We are not here to answer your questions! We are here to learn."

Eli turned to Dave and me and said, "Did he just say what I think he said?" All Dave could manage through his laughter was, "Shiiittttttttt" in his unmistakable Georgia drawl. I just looked at Eli and, biting my lip, nodded. It was all I could do to keep from laughing until the students were dismissed. Tom was annoyed with both sides and stood there shaking his head. Wayne, well, he did what Wayne does; he shrugged his shoulders and asked if there were any more questions.

Dave and I had bonded, pretty much from week one, and this "cultural event" solidified our friendship. We had similar senses of humor, didn't take ourselves too seriously, and we both had a love for cats, Thai food, and watching movies.

After class was over for the day and Eli, Dave, and I had made sure things were picked up around the track, we headed to Tom's office to debrief on the day's training—and to rehash the hilarious story. But when we got there, Tom was in no mood for a joke.

"Fuck them!" He was beet red and staring at his phone when we walked in. Wayne was already sitting across from him. I looked to Wayne for a clue about what was going on, but he just shrugged back at me.

"Fuck. Them," Tom repeated, opening his unclenched fist and letting out a loud exhale.

Apparently, Wayne had had some trouble with the people at the shooting range earlier that week. He was trying to solidify the details for the weapons training for the Kazakhs, but the guys who ran the range weren't cooperating. At first Wayne had thought it was just a scheduling mix-up. "I told him I'd just talk to Tom and get it sorted out," Wayne told us. "Then the guy says, 'Yeah, you VIP guys make so much money, why don't you just rent your own range?'"

I could see Tom heating up again as he launched into the story of what had happened after that.

"First of all, I told them, all this guy does is teach firearms. That's just one facet of our program, so yeah, he makes less than us. Second, I straightened them out. I talked to the head asshole at Wackenhut"— Wackenhut was the private company that the State Department con-tracted to run much of the ATA program—"and told them there's no room for this professional jealousy bullshit. This ain't a schoolyard." This was the first of many not-so-pleasant encounters with Wackenhut and other individuals affiliated with the ATA program.

By the time they graduated, the Kazakh delegation had warmed up to us. During the graduation lunch, they acknowledged each in-structor, one by one, saying a few words about each of us and then presenting us with a gift from their country. Finally, they came to me, and the head of the delegation said, "Last but definitely not least, Miss Mary Beth." He went on to talk about how "unique" it was for them to experience a woman as a trainer and how I had "masculine qualities" in my style. At this point, Dave was nudging me on my left, cracking up, and my eyes were nearly popping out of my head. The delegation leader then presented me with their gift. It was a whip. A whip with a handle made out of a deer hoof.

"Mary," he said, "we are giving you this gift because you need to keep your fellow instructors, your future students, and your future husband under control, and this will help." The whole room broke out in laughter. I am pretty sure my face was red, but, because so few of the groups we trained had ever worked with women, never mind being trained by one, this wasn't the only awkward moment I'd endure.

Eventually, I'd have my own problems with the Wackenhut asshole. He was a retired Air Force general who clearly had issues with a female in any role other than secretary or housewife. He was not shy about his chauvinistic views, and I'd been warned several times about things he'd said. He attempted to stir up trouble with our ATA program supervisor by saying, "Well, Will, how do you like it that *that woman*, Mary Beth Wilkas, is making more money than you?"

I was, in fact, not making more money than Will. This petty, classless Wackenhut-hired individual was trying to stir the pot and get me tossed from the team because, in his backwards view, women belonged in the kitchen, barefoot and pregnant.

Thankfully, Mike Harris had our back, as usual, and he ran interference. I had moments where I was annoyed at the whole situation, but I was grateful to Mike for taking it off of my hands, and more important, for allowing me to focus on what mattered. I was proud to be where I was. I was the only female instructor in any of the ATA courses being conducted in Albuquerque, and there were between eight and ten courses being taught there, depending on the year and the month. In fact, I was told that I was the first and only female instructor in the history of the ATA program.

• • •

We had heard a story from another one of the ATA courses being taught in Albuquerque that gave us a perspective on the foreign cultures we'd encounter with our delegations. A student from a Middle Eastern country, while shopping in town after a day of training, allegedly stole something from a big box store and was caught by the store's security. As a result, he was sent home to his country. The ATA later found out that he was hanged—not for the crime, per se, but rather for disgracing their country while in the US in an official capacity.

The reactions of the macho military and law-enforcement men from the different cultures that sent delegations varied widely from class to class. Having the respect of my fellow instructors made a huge difference as to how the students perceived and treated me. One thing that was fascinating for me to watch was how the students' responses to me changed: on day one, their reception was often chilly, but they warmed to me more and more as the days passed. I did not take this treatment personally; it reflected how women were perceived in the field of security in most of the rest of the world. Hell, many men I trained and worked with in the United States felt women had no place in the industry. With very few exceptions, however, the students were extremely respectful of me, acknowledging both my knowledge and my enthusiasm for teaching.

Standing in Mike Harris's huge office at the ATA building, a feeling of déjà vu came over me. Like my colleague Wayne, Mike Harris had worked in the USSS under six presidents, from Nixon to Clinton, before he retired, and his office was decorated with USSS paraphernalia and photos of presidents, especially Ronald Reagan.

I was in his office taking advantage of what he'd told us was an open-door policy because I wanted to get ahead of a situation I'd seen in the schedule. A delegation from Saudi Arabia had just been slated to come in for training in a couple of months. "As a female, I just don't think I'll be effective with this group, sir," I said, finishing my appeal.

"Mary Beth?" Mike began, rising to his feet. Taking in the fifty-ish, six-foot-tall man in his dark suit—he had just come back from a meeting with some Wackenhut folks—I almost felt like I was speaking with the Agent in Charge at WFO.

"Yes, sir?"

"Just call me Mike, Mary Beth."

"Yes, sir. Um, Mike. I just think it makes sense that I should sit this round of training out. I don't see me, as a female, being effective with this group. It's not really about me, right? This is about the students learning. I mean, women aren't even allowed to drive in their country. What's going to happen on the track? I'm OK to sit out."

For a split second, Mike looked like he might think about it.

Instead, he said something I would not have heard from my boss at WFO: "Fuck 'em. This is our country. If they don't like it, it's their problem."

"Roger that, sir. I mean, Mike," I said, my eyes practically bulging out of their sockets.

"Mary Beth, you know, I was at the track the other day, and somebody mentioned you." *Shit. Was this how things were going to be here? People gossiping and reporting on each other?* "He said he saw you demo the slalom on Tuesday." The slalom—driving as fast as you could through cones spaced sixty feet apart—was the most difficult thing we tackled on the track. You had a margin of error of about two miles an hour and maybe an eighth of an inch rotation on the steering wheel.

"He said he saw you clear the whole thing while casually instructing two students in the back seat the entire time. He was impressed."

Mike sat back down, and I could tell the conversation was coming to a close. "Our country is offering the Saudis an opportunity. If they don't like getting instruction from one of our best people, who happens to be a woman, they can go home."

"Roger that, sir. Thank you, sir."

The Saudi Arabian students were quiet, but attentive. During the first class I taught, Walking Formations, I sent the students on a break and was up in the front of the room reviewing the next section.

"Excuse me?" It was one of the students. "I have a question."

The Saudi student asked his question and then stood there looking at me and waiting for an answer. I looked over my right shoulder, then my left, thinking, "No way is he asking ME a question." Wrong. He just stood there, stared at me, and waited for his answer. I was so taken aback that I had to ask him to please repeat his question. The next three weeks with that delegation proved my assumptions about them wrong. They were good students and respectful of me as a female, and I enjoyed learning about their culture.

I remember that graduation ceremony well; on one side of the podium were the instructors and on the other was the brass—representatives from ATA in DC, local ATA higher-ups, and Wackenhut managers. We cringed a little when Mike Harris got to his famous line, giving us a little smirk. As he said, "Yet another iteration of this course done perfectly perfect," I could see a twinge of annoyance on the Wackenhut asshole's face. Of course, we knew Mike enunciated the "perfectly perfect" especially for him, just to stir the pot a bit. The tension was building between the Wackenhut asshole, other Albuquerque-based ATA folks and our team so Mike was letting them know he had our backs. Thank you, Mike.

The post-9/11 climate continued to be intense, and it wasn't uncommon for the head of a delegation to address it. On the first day of their class, a colonel from India spoke to all of us and said, "First of all, as a representative of my country, we would like to say we're very sorry for what your country has gone through." When we got to the unit called Terrorist Operations, I got teary-eyed when Tom showed pictures of and spoke about what had happened at the Twin Towers, the Pentagon, and Somerset County, Pennsylvania.

When Pakistan was slated to be trained with us through ATA in VIP Protection, we were told to keep the news "hush hush." The higher ups in the State Department in Washington, DC, wanted to avoid having a massive press presence overshadowing the training in Albuquerque. Unfortunately, the delegation did not have an easy time while en route to our training center in Albuquerque; in fact, they were removed by security from an American airline. On their flight from London to the United States, a flight attendant had "concerns about the presence of such a large group of Middle Eastern–looking men on the flight." All eighteen members of the delegation had to deplane. The airline later apologized, once it was confirmed they were traveling to the United States at the invitation of the US government. Awkward, for sure, but the students were amazingly understanding about the incident, and we were able to discuss it with them during their training.

To the chagrin of people like the Wackenhut asshole, the VIP Protection course quickly became the most requested course under ATA. There was actually a waiting list for the course that was quite long, and it was a big deal for a delegation to receive a spot in the program. That's why it was such a shock when we learned that not one, but five groups from Colombia had been given back-to-back slots to be trained. This happened, we were told, because Álvaro Uribe, then the president of Colombia, was the only leader in South America that willingly "assisted" the United States in those first few months after 9/11 and beyond. For that, he and his administration were being rewarded.

Ballistic glass, also called bullet-resistant glass, is a material that's both incredibly strong and incredibly flexible. When you first fire on it, it might crack but it won't shatter. But even the toughest material can only take so much abuse. If you keep firing round after round against even the highest level of ballistic glass, it's eventually going to break.

I'd never worked on a team with such a phenomenal dynamic, excellent skills, and broad experience before; we had the full support of an outstanding regional manager, Mike Harris, too. Our team in Albuquerque should have been golden. But unfortunately, though perhaps inevitably, cracks eventually started to show.

Tragically, in February of 2003, Mike Harris passed away from a heart attack while in Athens, Greece, on an official US government visit with another ATA employee. They were doing some advance work for the 2004 Summer Olympics. It was truly a terrible loss of a good man and a loyal friend.

With his loss, we also realized how much Mike had shielded us from. Suddenly, it started to feel like every time the I's on a form were dotted wrong someone on our team, usually me, was getting reamed for it. The latest problem was the use of cell phone minutes. Apparently I was spending too much time on the phone talking to actors. In a program that was spending millions of taxpayer dollars, the fact that my cell phone bill was five dollars over the monthly plan was somehow an issue.

On the last day of each VIP Protection course, a final training exercise was coordinated in and around Albuquerque. This entailed the students serving as protection agents for a VIP with a busy and dangerous one-day schedule. The activity began with the VIP, a local actor, arriving at a private airport—we used a real jet sitting on the runway at a fixed-based operator that was thrilled to add some excitement to their otherwise uneventful days. The agents then transported the VIP to a variety of locations in town, according to the schedule they were given. During this exercise, we created endless challenges for the students based on the training they had received over the previous three weeks. This included a variety of "attacks" on the VIP that the students were expected to thwart. I was responsible for all of the preparations for the day-long exercise. I hired the actors, organized the different teams of "terrorists," and coordinated with the Albuquerque police, the fixed-base operator, and all of the other locations we put on the VIP's itinerary. So, sure, the cellphone minutes added up, but it's not like I was making personal phone calls.

Tom came to me about it first, saying, "Mary Beth, we gotta talk. You are gonna be pissed. Hell, I'm pissed." But I could tell—Tom made no secret of it—that he didn't want to waste time talking about it. Within minutes he'd end up getting angry, but not at me. "That Wackenhut asshole, again." And despite the fact that that blockhead had somehow gotten promoted, he continued to stir things up for our team. This time, having me questioned for spending five dollars over my allotted phone plan.

What made me crazy was that, at the same time we were getting hammered left and right, the VIP Protection program—made up of the same Fantastic Five from day one plus one late addition—continued to receive nonstop praise and commendations from the bosses at the State Department. So when someone was sent down from DC—a subject matter expert—to review our course, we didn't know what to expect. As it turned out, after taking in three weeks of our instruction, the subject matter expert didn't have a lot of feedback for us. He said, "I've never said this to any other team of instructors before. You guys are showing us how things should be done, not the other way around. Just keep doing what you're doing!"

And yet, there I was, sitting in a meeting with our program supervisor on Wackenhut's side and, I guess, whoever the person was in charge of counting cell phone minutes. Tom sat next to me fuming.

Maybe I had less patience than I once had. Or maybe I'd been in the private sector for too long and had just forgotten what it was like dealing with the bullshit, the layers upon layers of bureaucracy.

Miraculously, the "issue" got resolved, and they agreed, after what to this day seems like a comical debate, to spend the whopping five dollars more per month on upgrading my phone plan. Before we left the ATA building that day, I wasn't able to stop myself from asking the Wackenhut manager a question.

"All of this for five dollars, Will. Really?" I just shook my head. *Aren't we all on the same side?* I was genuinely mystified.

Shortly after Mike's death, Tom left our team and took a position in Bogotá, Colombia, working under the auspices of the US Embassy. Soon after, I decided I was going to take a break from the next VIP Protection course, head to Europe for a few weeks, and think about my next professional move. As amazing as this ATA team was, I was getting that itch—the need for my next challenge. Plus, the Wackenhut offensive was not backing down. They continued to harass our team, and without someone to run interference, they would eventually succeed in taking one of us out.

During what was the most pivotal time in US history, at least in my lifetime, I truly felt honored to be part of something that mattered and that moved international relations forward. In total, I worked eighteen months as an instructor with the ATA VIP Protection program, and I helped train fifteen delegations from Bangladesh, Kazakhstan, Sri Lanka, Pakistan, Nepal, Saudi Arabia, Spain, Uzbekistan, India, Greece, Azerbaijan, Malaysia, and Colombia.

Instead of teaching at the next VIP Protection course, I met two girlfriends in Greece, and then we flew to Tuscany and met up with a couple of our guy friends. That's where I was when I got a message that Tom had called from Colombia. When I called him back, he told me the new program he was working with was looking for a unicorn.

"Yeah, Mary Beth, a unicorn. I'm in our Monday morning briefing and my boss walks in and says he's looking for a unicorn. We all laughed. He went on to ask if anyone knew—are you ready for this?—a female who's fluent in Spanish, a former federal agent, preferably former State Department or Secret Service, has extensive international experience, and is willing to come to Bogotá, Colombia?"

"Well, Tom, that sounds like me. Except for one thing."

"What's that?"

"I've got a master's in forensic psychology too."

"Oh, Christ."

CHAPTER
11

BOGOTÁ, COLOMBIA
2003

"What the hell, Mary Beth! Are you nuts?"

It had been a while since I'd heard that from my mother, at least the way she was saying it now on the phone, like she really meant it. I was back in San Diego, getting ready to head to Bogotá when she'd called. I knew we'd have to talk about the job sooner or later, but I'd been avoiding the topic.

"Mom," I said, trying to soften the blow. "It's only for sixty days, and Tom's already down there, and—"

"I don't care about Tom, Mary Beth. I care about you!"

I might not have settled down, exactly, after getting my master's degree in New York, but I knew that for the past few years my mother had been happy that I hadn't been heading off on missions in countries where bombings and witch burnings were daily occurrences.

Naturally, I didn't tell her that three months earlier Colombia had experienced the worst terrorist attack it had endured in over a decade. On February 7, 2003, 26-year-old squash instructor and club member John Freddy Arellan arrived at the thirteen-story El Nogal social and business club in his red Renault Megane. Although El Nogal was said to have stringent security, Arellan's car, which was full of approximately two hundred kilograms of ANFO explosives, passed a security inspection. Reportedly, the Renault had been modified to hold the explosives in the engine firewall. Arellan's vehicle was detonated, with him in it, as the vehicle was being parked on the third floor, killing thirty-eight people and wounding over two hundred more.

"It's a great opportunity," I told her. "I know you don't want me back in the field, but this is what I was trained to do, Mom, and this is an amazing opportunity."

On February 13, 2003, at approximately the same time I had been offered the position in Bogotá, three Americans had been kidnapped. Marc Gonsalves, Tom Howes, and Keith Stansell were three US contractors on a drug surveillance mission in a cocaine-producing jungle when their plane crash-landed in guerrilla territory. The American pilot and a Colombian intelligence officer traveling on the same mission were shot and killed by the Revolutionary Armed Forces of Colombia (FARC). The three American captives were forced to march with the guerrillas deeper and deeper into the jungle.

"Mom, you know I can take care of myself."

Colombia, at the time, had the distinction of earning the moniker "the kidnap capitol of the world." Things were considered dangerous enough for US citizens that the State Department issued an official Level 3 (Orange) Travel Advisory—Reconsider Travel, discouraging Americans from traveling to and around Colombia. The highest warning is Level 4 (Red)—Do Not Travel; it is generally seen with countries such as Iraq, Iran, Afghanistan, Syria, Central African Republic, and North Korea.

Bogotá, Escuela de Caballeria Firearms Range, 2004

"And it's not like I'll be on my own. I'll be working under the auspices of the US Embassy, within the Regional Security Office." I kept to myself that I would be working with the leadership in Colombia who were at war with several groups, including the AUC (United Self-Defense Forces of Colombia) and the ELN (National Liberation Army). They were also, of course, at war with the FARC, at the time the most prolific and dangerous terrorist group in the country.

"I promise, as soon as the contract is up, I'll come and visit you and Dad in Huntley." After ten years, my parents had moved back to the Chicago area from South Carolina.

When I hung up, I went back to packing my suitcase, but I kept picturing my mother turning to my father and sighing, at her wits end, scared, again, for me.

"Check out the latest," Tom said as he tossed the day's newspaper at me before he started the car. I buckled into the passenger seat and took in the front page. A photo showed a beautiful, dark-haired, aristocratic-looking woman, maybe forty-five years old, crowded by a gaggle of squinting uniformed men, their insignia-laden caps larger than their heads. The accompanying article detailed the guerrillas latest attempt on the life of the woman, Marta Lucía Ramírez, Colombia's new minister of defense (MOD) and the principal of my mission.

My briefing on the MOD taught me that she was considered to be under a higher threat than any other member of the Colombian government at the time. She was part of the Álvaro Uribe administration, which automatically meant she was an enemy of the guerillas and the *narcotraficantes*. And, as MOD, she was a prime mover—and a prime target—in the fight against the FARC that the president had campaigned on. If that wasn't enough, she'd been vocal about her determination to stop the long-standing corruption that existed within the Colombian military, meaning many of the very powerful people working "under" her in the military hierarchy wanted her gone.

Tom pulled away from the curb at Bogotá's El Dorado Airport as I read on. "Trying to kill her and Uribe is like the national pastime down here," he said. "Welcome to Colombia."

Ambassador Anne Patterson rushed into her office in the US Embassy where we'd been waiting, apologizing for being late. As she sized me up, I got the distinct feeling that I wasn't what she was expecting.

"I'm sorry, Ms. Wilkas, but there's just no way that you're *retired* Secret Service," she said.

Retired? Even if I'd stayed, I'd have needed just under fifteen years before I could retire, almost twenty for maximum benefits.

In her blue skirt suit and chin-length blond hair, the ambassador looked to be about ten years older than me. Still, I couldn't help myself from blurting out a defense.

"I'm not *that* old!"

The room was silent for a moment, and then the ambassador laughed. We all—me, Tom, the deputy chief of mission, and Mark Hunter, the regional security officer (RSO) and also my new boss—followed suit.

"Ma'am," Mark Hunter spoke up, "Mary Beth is former Secret Service. She left the agency in the nineties and has been working on State Department and other contracts ever since."

"That makes more sense," the ambassador said. She looked me in the eye, and I smiled back as she continued. "I know how that job has a way of pushing good people out."

And then, suddenly, she was right to business. "Listen. Mary Beth, as you know, your mission here is not to function as a protection agent."

I did know that, but it was good to hear it confirmed. In the few days I'd been in country, I'd gotten the sense that Tom hadn't been able to help himself from expanding his role. I knew how passionate Tom was about his work, so it was no surprise that he'd begun to protect the president when he saw a need. I, on the other hand, had every intention of sticking to the brief I was handed.

"As part of the Presidential Security Program, you'll observe and advise security details in tandem with Tom. You'll be responsible for the minister of defense and vice president of Colombia, and the mayor of Bogotá."

I said nothing, but my operating principle—never let them see you sweat—was being tested. If we were sticking to the brief, the job description I'd been handed was to observe and advise on the MOD's security. One person. Not three. Hadn't that been why they were looking so hard for a woman to fill the role? To give the female MOD some room to breathe in the world of Latin American machismo? Maybe my time in Albuquerque had made me too suspicious of the State Department and its bureaucracy, but I hadn't come all the way to Colombia to be set up to fail. But then Ambassador Patterson really surprised me. She acknowledged the challenge and laid out a solid plan of action.

"We all recognize that Marta Lucía is a full-time job. She may even be at higher risk than the president depending on the day and the intelligence coming our way. So I'm just going to ask you for one month. Do your best to cover all three of them. Then, write me an official cable describing the security demands of each principal and asking for another security advisor. I will approve another security advisor to take over the vice president and the mayor. Then your focus will be solely on the minister of defense. I just need some solid documentation to send to the secretary to justify an addition to your team."

When she said the secretary, I realized she meant Condoleezza Rice, the US secretary of state. That certainly made the promise more credible. It also made me a bit more nervous. I admired the secretary, and I probably felt less prepared to write a diplomatic cable that she'd read than I did doing the job of two—hell, three—security advisors.

The deputy chief rose from the couch, but the ambassador stayed in her seat. I guess that was it for our meeting. I couldn't shake the feeling that I was getting screwed, like I'd been brought here under false pretenses. As Tom followed Mark and the deputy chief out of the door, I

Tocancipá race track, Antiterrorism Driving and Motorcade Operations training, 2004

walked toward the ambassador's desk, leaned in, and reached out my hand.

"Thank you, Mary Beth," she said, looking me in the eye and shaking the hand I'd offered. "Remember, write me that cable and I'll get you your third advisor."

"Thank you, Ambassador." For the time being I had no choice but to trust her.

On a sunny day like the one we were experiencing, much of the countryside in Colombia's Antioquia Department was dominated by views of the Andes. Tom and I had been on dirt roads for at least thirty minutes as we made our way from the city of Medellín, driving past rolling hills, short, dense groves of palms and pines, whitewashed houses, and even the occasional plaster shrine to some saint. Eventually the car pulled into a short drive on a large but tidy piece of property. There was grass as far as you could see and, beyond it, more blue mountains. In front of us was a modest ranch house. You wouldn't have guessed that it belonged to the nation's president.

I heard the shouts before we got out of our car.

"Who's got the six? Cover the six!"

Tom actually relaxed a bit and smiled as a hand pounded on the roof. I grabbed for the door and jumped outside.

"Eduardo!" I hugged my former student from the ATA program in Albuquerque.

"Hahaha! Maribel!" He was wearing a dark suit—his best Secret Service look—and smiling widely. "I haven't forgotten, cover the six, right?"

I had really been a pain in the ass with them in class about that. We'd watched the video of Yitzhak Rabin's assassination over and over again, and I'd drill them on what all had gone wrong. Rabin's assassin had walked right up to him and shot him in the back of the head. I had to smile now, satisfied that at least some of my training had stuck. It was something that I hoped would make my job in Colombia easier. I'd personally trained three of the five groups from Colombia that had passed through Albuquerque. The fact that seventy-two agents here already knew me as an effective, bilingual instructor and professional would be a major advantage in a place that was notoriously chauvinistic. Eduardo was a shift leader for President Uribe's security detail. He told me that he'd already spoken highly of me to the president. I was grateful, and I was bowled over by the warm greetings I received from him and the other former students protecting the president and vice president.

I made a mental note that, though we'd been waved onto the driveway by a guard with a Beretta 9mm pistol and an Uzi strapped on his person, there was no physical barrier, no gate, at the entrance to the ranch, just a break in the long 2×4 fence. That would end up near the top of the long list of observations I'd make in this assessment of the security measures in place here. But before we started to really dive into the project, Eduardo led us past a small white outbuilding that I guessed would house the detail's command post to the house where President Uribe was waiting to greet us.

It was clear, as he showed us around, that the president was proud of his ranch property. It was also clear to me that it would be a challenge to protect. It was sprawling and wide open, and a large span of it was close to the road. Uribe and his family had owned it for years before he'd won the presidency, and I could tell they wouldn't be keen on the idea of having their freedom restricted. When the tour was over, we thanked President Uribe, he returned to his home, and we turned to Eduardo.

Now I pulled my clipboard, my pen, and my camera from my brief-case.

"OK," Tom said. "Give us the lay of the land from your perspective."

Eduardo walked us through what his team had in place as far as pro-tecting the physical buildings and then President Uribe, his wife, and his children when they were there. I took note of what they did have in place and made far more exhaustive observations of the tremendous amount of security they *didn't* have in place, particularly in light of the number of assassination attempts against Uribe.

The white building we'd seen when we arrived was, indeed, the command post. On closer inspection it seemed to have been hastily put up just to house the security agents, their equipment, the keys to the security vehicles, and chargers for the radios—very old radios. There were no cameras. No system to log the comings and goings of the president's family, or anyone else for that matter.

"Maribel, I know we are lacking security here, but to ask the president for these things . . ." His detail wasn't being funded the way it should have been, and it was difficult, if not impossible, to shift that mentality because of the culture of bureaucracy and power dynamics in Colombia. Never mind the fact that Uribe was very much "a man of the people," and his humility and reputation would not allow the country's money to be spent on his security. Eduardo was a trusted long-time aide to the president, but he still didn't feel empowered to make expensive material requests.

"Eduardo, what do you think you need to make this work?" I asked.

I met the MOD at her office, a large wood-paneled room filled with neat stacks of paperwork. Besides the MOD, a uniformed member of the army stood in the room. He hadn't been part of our training in Albuquerque; if he had been, I hoped he would have known that his post was outside the door, not inside with his protectee.

"Anne told me she was sending a Secret Service agent." It made sense that she'd be on good terms with Ambassador Patterson. "But I understand you are no longer with them. Tell me, Maribel. What is your background?"

OK, fair enough, I thought. I knew I wasn't the first contractor that had come from the embassy. And she was surrounded by people she rightfully could not trust. I went over my credentials. By the time I was done, it seemed like I had bored her guard. I followed the MOD's gaze to the corner of the room, where the guard was sitting on one of the black file cabinets, eyeballing his shoe. I figuratively shook my head, beginning to understand that I was going to have a lot to do to shape things up here.

"Very impressive, Maribel. I imagine you are aware of the threats against me?"

"I am, Ministra," I answered. "And I am confident that I can assist you, with the support of the US Embassy. I know you have a town hall visit coming up in Barranquilla, and I'd like to accompany you." What I didn't say was "to assess your security." This was for two reasons: one, the MOD knew what my role was and, two, I did not want the guard in her office to hear what I had to say. I had no idea, at the time, who was who, and who, if anyone, I could trust.

"I'd also like to review the security at your home here in Bogotá, if you'll allow me. Perhaps we can put some additional measures in place to—"

"Harden the target?" the MOD casually asked. I was going to say "make you feel safer," but she was right. The MOD was far more knowledgeable and aware than many gave her credit for. To me, this was one of her strong points, especially operating in a landscape of wily military higher-ups.

The president's ranch had been a good place for my first assessment. I knew that I could trust Eduardo to be completely honest about what he needed, and that made it easier for me when it came to writing my first official purchase request, one of hundreds I would write over the two and a half years I ended up working in Colombia.

After that first mission, I spent hours in my cubicle writing. The first order of business was the after action report, which boiled down to three sections: positive observations, negative observations, and recommendations. This was followed by an official write-up of the security survey we'd done on the president's ranch in Medellín. Tom and I shared that massive task. Finally, I got to the purchase requests.

The ranch was in a rustic area, not far from both FARC strongholds and areas where the citizens weren't necessarily pro-Uribe. It was vulnerable. At first, Tom and I wrote a list of what was needed equipment-wise, what I would have expected to see in a detail with resources like the USSS or, say, a wealthy family like the Darts. Then I took another look at what I had written and started paring down. What would really be realistic here?

I smiled this time when we were stopped, a freshly painted 2×4 barring our way down the dirt drive. Eduardo's man at the gate to the president's ranch had us roll down the windows and identify ourselves. When we proceeded through and greeted Eduardo at the white security hut, we congratulated him for the changes he'd made.

Then it was his turn to smile as he inspected the cargo in the back of our armored Ford SUV.

"Oh my god, Maribel! Tom!"

He was like a kid on Christmas, scanning the boxes of computers, custom ballistic vests, and digital cameras, as well as some much-needed office supplies. When Tom tossed him the keys to the Ford, I thought he might cry.

The MOD acknowledged me at the air base, but just barely. In her yellow scarf and blue dress, she stood out in the crowd of uniforms and suits. I was accompanying her, along with probably twenty-five or thirty other people, to Barranquilla, where she'd hold a town meeting.

It was hot, so we all—reporters, advisors, generals—were sweating in the open room, milling about as we waited for the plane to take us out of Bogotá. I thought I heard someone whisper something about the "American embassy girl." It felt like I was at a cocktail party where I didn't know anyone. Except without the cocktails.

Finally the crowd started to filter out of the room and onto the tarmac. I took the opportunity to step back and watch—keeping an eye on the minister's security, looking for a familiar face, maybe the assistant from her office. Instead, as everyone else shuffled to the plane, I spotted a flash of yellow—the MOD's scarf— as she turned and looked at me.

Had she been observing me? How I was conducting myself in the waiting room? I would have been if I were her, trying to suss out whether I knew my job, if I had her interests at heart, if I could be trusted. I was the last one to board the huge cargo plane, finding a seat for the bumpy hour-long ride to Barranquilla.

From Barranquilla we were driven to a tiny, dusty village, where tables had been set up in the town square against the backdrop of some low buildings and, beyond them, the sea. The MOD was there to give a speech and then have a Q&A with the people in the town, talk about their fears, the threats from the narcos and the FARC. The mayor of the town was talking the minister's ear off, and I found a place to watch from a discreet vantage point. The protection agents who'd come with us and were responsible for the MOD's security were walking around and chatting with each other, the drivers were sleeping under trees, and the head of the security team was pouring himself a glass of lemonade.

"Hello, my name is General Roma. You are Maribel?"

I knew the name, though I hadn't met Roma before. Sunglasses, uniform, and a big grin, like the Grinch. He was the general who was actually responsible for the unit tasked with guarding—or not—the MOD.

"You work with the US Embassy?"

"I do, General."

I turned to face him and then took two steps to the side. Now, I was out of the shade, but I was looking directly at the MOD. Roma turned to face me, his back to the square—and his charge.

"And how are things going with you and Marta Lucía?"

"Well. Thank you, General." I didn't know the rules, but I knew there was a game being played here.

"And what is your opinion of my men, Marta Lucía's security?"

"I have been in country only a short time, General. It's too early for me to share my observations."

"Ah, very good. Well, I am sure the US Embassy has chosen an excellent advisor to help Marta Lucía."

Though I could tell he was skeptical of my abilities, he continued buddying up to me as his soldiers, Marta Lucía's protection agents, cooled themselves in the shade and the head of security continued drinking glass after glass of lemonade.

"Are you concerned about the threats to the minister, General?" I asked, as he turned to walk away.

"Ah, Marta Lucía." He pointed over his shoulder—in the wrong direction. "She is a strong woman."

I didn't like his condescending and dismissive tone. It was clear he was used to his power intimidating people and he didn't think my skills, Marta Lucía, or this mission were worth taking seriously. This was one of the only things I left out of my report on the trip.

On November 15, 2003, around 10:30 p.m. on a Saturday, suspected FARC rebels threw grenades into two crowded bars in Bogotá's Zona Rosa, or "Pink Zone," a posh and popular district frequented by Americans that was just two blocks from my apartment. I received a call from a colleague at the US Embassy approximately two minutes after the attacks. I subsequently got my weapon and ammunition ready, got dressed (I was in my pajamas), and met Tom on the scene to offer our assistance.

We knew it was not smart to rush to the scene of an attack. Terrorists, if they are well prepared and smart, will often use the initial attack, in this case two grenades, to gather as many people as possible to the scene. Then they launch a second attack. Maximum carnage is the goal. Eventually, in the same breath we were thanked, Tom and I would get scolded for showing up there.

The attacks killed one Colombian woman and injured seventy-two others, including four Americans, two of whom were American Airlines pilots. Local authorities and the US Embassy determined the FARC were responsible and the motivation for the grenade attacks was to directly target and hurt Americans who frequented the area and were, thus, considered supporters of President Uribe.

I had no plans to share any of this information with my parents; I did not want to make them worry or, worse, start another argument with my mother about me "having to come home."

However, shortly after I returned to my apartment from the attack scene, I turned on the TV and saw that CNN was reporting on the attacks. Shit. Now, for sure my parents would find out.

Although it was late, I called my parents' home, and my mother answered. I gave her the CNN version of the incidents and assured her that I was safe and sound.

Surprisingly, she sounded totally relaxed. Apparently she was watching coverage of the incidents on TV at that very moment.

"Thanks for calling, honey. Your sister, Anne, called after seeing the story on TV and told me not to worry about you because the attacks were at a nightclub and you never go to nightclubs." I laughed—it was absolutely true. What my mother did not know was that the two trendy bars that were targeted were not nightclubs but actually places I had been to several times before. But there was no way I was going to clarify that little detail.

I spent my days running around, going from various sites with the vice president and his security team to the mayor's motorcades and town hall meetings to meetings with the MOD to the countryside. But my job entailed more than that; I was also tasked with writing reports and cables. It was a relentless pace that continued pretty much throughout most of the mission; luckily as a contractor, I was allowed to work and get paid up to sixty hours per week.

Bogotá, 2003

I would brief the embassy on the highlights and concerns related to my missions, and then I would send weekly cables back to DC, relating a version of the same. I also wrote up mission status reports, which went to the RSO, our operational boss. These reports detailed the past, present, and future of our mission—where we had been, where we were, and where we intended to go. Mission status reports essentially mapped the entirety of our whole program from start to finish, and we discussed them at length on a bimonthly basis with the RSO.

Finally, I wrote the requisite cable to the US secretary of state, and the ambassador gave her approval for a third individual to join our team and take over the duties related to the vice president and the mayor of Bogotá as a US security advisor. When it came down to it, Tom and I pretty much had complete autonomy to hire the person we wanted for the role; we just had to get approval from our boss, the RSO.

When we walked into our meeting with the RSO to make our case, we were shocked at his response: "Sure. You have made me look good so far." I waited for the "But . . . ," but it never came. He trusted us, and he trusted we would bring in the right guy.

That was it. In the end, of course, red tape being red tape, it did take a couple of months to actually process the addition to the team, but it happened. At that point, I was free to focus solely on the MOD. It was amazing to see what we could accomplish when the government, at least the people we were working for, put their faith in us. It definitely made the time and work of drafting cables and reports, working and reworking budgets, and spending endless hours in the field feel like it was worth it.

Our third advisor was in place by the time an intriguing out-of-town site visit with the MOD was scheduled, and I wanted to be on this one—she was heading to FARC territory. Marta Lucía was now my only responsibility, and I knew she had decided she could trust me. However, as far as I had observed and from what I had heard from my internal sources, the recommendations I had been making to the MOD's head of security had fallen on deaf ears.

After we deplaned, I was able to jump into the motorcade's follow car. We were on the road with the windows up. I knew—and somehow the security detail didn't—that if an incident occurred, precious moments would be lost fumbling to roll the windows down before a weapon could be fired out of it.

What was worse was that the driver was doing nothing that I would call motorcade driving. Our car was directly behind the minister's, in a sleek row, as if we were just two cars in traffic. Plus, he was way too close to the bumper of the vehicle transporting the MOD.

As a follow vehicle, you should always be protecting the vehicle that the protectee is in. If the protectee's vehicle is in the right lane, as the follow car, you're straddling, at an angle, two lanes—the right lane and the one to the left of it—to be on the offensive and keep people away from that car. That's how we did it in the USSS and in Haiti. Hell, that's how we did it everywhere. You're aggressive. You're actually protecting someone. You're shoving cars out of the way because you are an official motorcade, and it's obvious you're an official motorcade.

But this guy wasn't driving like a follow car should. He must have thought his job was just to transport agents to the site. He was wrong, but I was coming to realize that I couldn't blame the individual agents. Besides the few guys within the Ministry of Defense who'd come to Albuquerque, the protection agents here had had zero training. Ever. Seeing as I had discussed all of these issues with the MOD's head of security on at least two occasions thus far, it was clear to me that he was just not listening. Or, more accurately, he just did not care.

I saw the same thing once we arrived at the site, an office building in a suburb. The advance man—well, he was supposed to be the advance man—walked side by side with the minister, holding the door for her as she entered the building. There was no concept of advance or formation at work. No real organization. No training.

I was starting to worry. Our reports at the embassy were all saying the same thing, hammering home the same point under the "negative observations" section: the protection agents for the MOD clearly had no training. They needed training as much as—more than—they needed armored cars, weapons, or ammo from the US government.

When we were on the tarmac, ready to head back to Bogotá, the MOD casually strolled up to my side.

"Maribel, when we board the plane, leave a seat open next to you, please." This trip, we were on a private plane, once belonging to the government of Colombia.

On board, before we took off, Marta Lucía got up from her seat, which was two rows back and across the aisle from her head of security, and joined me at the back of the plane.

The head of security watched her as she headed back to sit with me. Once he registered I was also watching him, he put on a "friendly" smile.

"Mary Beth"—the MOD had attended Harvard's Center for International Affairs, and she spoke English fluently, though rarely. "What is your opinion of my head of security?"

I said, "Why do you ask?" I was hesitant to point fingers or divulge what I sensed was going on.

"Well . . ." Marta Lucía hesitated for a few seconds, inhaled, and said, "I have to be honest; I don't trust him."

Was she testing me? Well, what the hell, what did I have to lose, besides a job?

"To be honest, although I've had very little exposure to him, I don't trust many people on your team yet, especially him. He is very lax in his duty to protect you. He doesn't take it seriously. He has not incorporated any of the changes I have suggested. And his attitude is trickling down to his soldiers."

She looked at me, and a knowing frown passed across her face while she shook her head.

"Gracias, Maribel."

"Marta Lucía, I have also seen him talking with some of the generals at various sites," I said, "and my intuition tells me he's reporting to them about you."

She just looked at me and nodded. It was as if I was simply confirming what she already knew. She rose from her seat.

"I'll be making some recommendations in my next report," I said. "This is not the first time, but I think I can find ways to increase your team's understanding of their role in your protection. I am confident things will change, Ministra."

Marta Lucía gave me a half smile, clearly unconvinced she would ever feel safe as the MOD.

• • •

I believe there were seventeen attempts on President Uribe's life while I was in Colombia. The latest had occurred when guerrillas placed explosives on a donkey on the president's motorcade route. It hadn't been caught by the police or the president's security detail; rather, it had unexpectedly exploded early, an hour before the president arrived in the town.

When we discussed these incidents at the embassy, we knew that, time after time, what had thwarted the constant threats and attacks wasn't security measures in place, or a well-executed advance, or good motorcade skills. It was luck.

We knew, too, that whatever training and good practices that people like Eduardo were able to instill would be lost soon. Every time a new president, mayor, or official came into office, the security team changed with them. No one trusted their predecessor's team. These protection agents served at the whim of their protectees. Plus, both the police protecting the president and the soldiers protecting the MOD commonly rotated out, all part of their career tracks. I'd seen agents and heads of security shift in and out of the MOD's office almost with each passing day. There was no such thing as institutional knowledge in security there.

The moment I finished writing to my parents, I knew it wouldn't be enough.

I'd started my email immediately after I'd seen the news, on March 31, 2004, that four Blackwater contractors were ambushed, killed, and hanged from a bridge in Fallujah, Iraq. It wasn't something I could keep from my mother. And though I was halfway around the world from Iraq, I knew it would make her think of me. I knew it would terrify her. As soon as I got back to my apartment at the end of the day, I dialed home.

My father answered.

"Hi, honey! How ya doing? Good. Okay, here's your mom." Typical dad, he wasn't much for the phone.

"Mom," I started, when she came on the line.

"Mary Beth, we just saw on the TV about those contractors—" I let her speak because I knew what I wanted to say was not going to go over so great.

"Listen, Mom. I need you and Dad to understand something. Please. I have everything I have ever asked for here. I have all the vehicles, weapons, ammunition, and equipment I need. So, God forbid, if anything ever happens to me, please know I willingly left my house every day to do my job."

For a moment she didn't say anything.

"That's not very reassuring, Mary Beth."

"Maybe, Mom. But I just needed to say it. Look, I just need you and Dad to know, I'm OK. And, if anything ever happens to me, please do not go after anyone. This was my choice."

One year after she took office, Marta Lucía Ramírez resigned her position as MOD. President Uribe accepted her resignation, and neither of them gave an explanation for her departure. A respected US-educated businessman, Jorge Alberto Uribe (no relation to the president), was named to replace her.

My first thought was, "Oh shit, there goes *my* job." Because a man was chosen as MOD after Marta Lucía resigned, I presumed that all of those involved would deem it more appropriate for a man to assume the security advisor role. I also contemplated the same issue—might a male advisor be a better fit for the job at this point? I knew the answer was no, but I wasn't sure everyone else involved would see it the same way.

On Sunday, the same day Marta Lucía resigned, the RSO called me and asked me to come to the embassy first thing on Monday for a meeting. At the meeting a few higher-ups assured me that my work thus far had been noteworthy, that our program was exceptional, and that I was staying put. And, according to them, everyone was on board with this decision, including the U.S. ambassador and the government of Colombia. I knew I was totally committed to this job and that I was working harder than ever before. Being acknowledged for it was flattering, and it fueled me to make our program even better.

Eventually, Tom, Tony (our newest security advisor), and I were made employees of the US State Department. The conversion from contractor status entailed a two-week processing period, and I took advantage of the opportunity to head home, starting my visit with a long-overdue trip to see my parents.

After dinner, we were sitting outside enjoying some wine when my mother cleared her throat. I knew what was coming—I was about to get my ass chewed.

"Mary Beth . . . you're not going back to Colombia," she said calmly.

I about choked on my wine.

"Mary Beth, you promised me after graduate school that you would leave this business."

"I'm sorry, Mom, but I never said that!"

I turned to my father. He looked thoughtful and stayed silent.

"Look, Mary Beth. I can't take this anymore. I just can't handle you gallivanting all over a dangerous country, wondering whether you are going to be kidnapped or killed. It's going to be the death of me!"

"Mom." How could I explain this to her? "I just became an employee of the State Department. I will be carrying a diplomatic passport, which gives me diplomatic immunity." She was not at all placated. "I've trained for this. I don't mean, like . . . yes, I am very well trained for what I do, but . . . This, this job. It is the thing that I've prepared for. For years. This is where I am supposed to be."

That wasn't what she had wanted to hear.

"You're not supposed to be someplace where you could die!"

Thinking back now, I realize that she was feeling helpless. Even then, I appreciated that she was concerned for me. But, at the same time, I was annoyed that I was almost forty years old and I felt like I had to convince my mother that I knew what I was doing. Did men ever have to do this?

"I can die anywhere, Mom!" Admittedly, this might not have been the thing to say to help my case. Then I added fuel to the fire. "OK, Mom. I'll just quit Colombia, head back to California, and get plowed into by a car while I'm buying organic basil at the farmer's market next Sunday." This had been an incident in the news in July 2003, less than two months after I had arrived in Colombia. An eighty-six-year-old man thought he was placing his foot on the brakes but, instead, hit the accelerator, slamming his car right into a farmer's market in Santa Monica. Ten people were killed, and sixty-three were injured.

"That's not the same thing, Mary Beth!" my mom practically screamed. "You are choosing to put yourself in harm's way."

"Mom, I believe in fate and just am not willing to live my life trying to avoid death. I can only promise that I will be as careful as I can."

My father finally stopped looking thoughtful and let out a sigh. "Lois, it's her life. We have to let her live it." I thought my mom might dump the rest of the wine in my father's lap, but she just sat there, frustrated and worried.

Before I headed back to Colombia, I stopped in San Diego for a week to see some friends and do some shopping. As I walked downtown, I realized that I had been keeping myself far from the curb, clinging to the buildings and shielding myself from the cars on the street, protecting myself from an explosion that, subconsciously, I knew was unlikely to come. Even in California my body was still holding on to the fear my brain had in Colombia that, on any given day, a bomb could go off in my neighborhood, on my block, next to me, across the street, anywhere.

Escuela de Caballería Firearms Range with MOD Agents, Bogotá, 2005

Ambassador-at-Large and Coordinator for Counterterrorism Cofer Black was coming to Colombia, and Tom and I would be giving him a presentation on our work, since our program's mission fell right into his purview.

Ambassador Patterson had been so pleased with our program that, beyond extending our employment with the embassy, she'd added a sizable chunk of money to our budget. It was the largest budget, by far, that I'd ever been responsible for managing, and it had gone extremely well. It was understandable for the State Department to want to hear what we'd done with their money, and we were happy to have the opportunity to discuss all that we had accomplished. After all, we were able to extend our program an entire year due to our efficient and responsible spending of the original budget. Almost unheard of.

Tom and I met in the embassy offices to discuss how we'd suggest using the money that was being made available to us. As the discussion spun out and we thought of the scale of our program, the same issue came up over and over: training. The Colombian agents needed formal training.

Tom and I had already been part of a team that had trained five groups of Colombians back in Albuquerque. However, at this point, not much more than a year later, many of those individuals were gone from their security teams—promoted, demoted, retired, or simply rotated out. It was part of Colombia's culture and mentality. They had no formal agencies 100 percent committed to the protection of certain individuals like we do in the US. Rather, security agents came and went as part of their career paths. That is, they often rotated in and out of a security team, staying a year or two before leaving for their next assignment. Or, the agents had been personally selected to be part of the team by the protectee because they had worked together in the past. Eduardo, for example, had been part of President Uribe's protection team since Uribe was the governor of Antioquia. It was unlikely that the next president would keep him on.

Tom said it. "What about creating a Colombian training academy?"

The idea was electric. As we discussed it more, we realized it was totally possible. We had the money in our budget; it was just being allocated to other line items. We quickly restructured our budget so that, during our meeting with Ambassador Cofer Black, we would be able to show that our program had the funds to follow through on our new project. In other words, our brilliant idea did not entail asking for any additional funds.

Next, we had to sell our idea to our operational boss. When we ran our idea by the RSO, thankfully, he was just as, if not more, excited as we were. "You guys are the best. Who else would come up with this amazing idea and want to take on the work to make it happen?"

We all knew this was an ambitious project for the US to take on in Colombia and that we had, at best, a 50/50 shot that Ambassador Cofer Black would approve our proposal, but we all agreed, as my mother would say, that "it never hurts to ask."

Before the meeting began, we met outside the conference room with one of Ambassador Cofer Black's aides. That was protocol. He told us how much time we had with the ambassador and asked us what we planned to talk about. When we shared that we were proposing a physical training academy, he looked at us and, without hesitating, said, "Yeah, that's not gonna happen—he won't approve that."

The same conference room at the embassy that we'd been in countless times before was transformed. The setup, with microphones at each seat and Tom, the RSO, and me facing the ambassador and one of his aides, reminded me of pictures I'd seen of the UN. After discussing the program's past accomplishments and what we were currently doing, the big moment arrived—the visiting ambassador asked us what we planned to do with the future of the program and how we planned to spend the remainder of our budget.

Tom began. "Well, Mr. Ambassador, we have a proposal for you."

For the next ten minutes or so, Tom, the RSO, and I took turns talking about our ambitious idea. The ambassador listened patiently, nodding his head every so often, but he said nothing. After we had finished with all of our talking points, the room was dead silent. The ambassador bowed his head for what seemed like forever. After a few minutes had passed, he looked up at us and said, "OK."

"OK?" I blurted out, beside myself.

"OK!" he responded, with a small smile.

We were stunned. The ambassador's aide sat there with his mouth open, also stunned, but in a different way. We walked out of that meeting with huge smiles on all of our faces. The RSO said to us, "Well, congratulations! That was pretty amazing. It looks like you guys have your work cut out for you. Now, go build that academy."

Purchasing millions of dollars of equipment was one thing; creating a facility that required a major shift in mentality, understanding, and operations in the military and police establishment of a foreign nation was another. But, hell, I loved a challenge, and this was a monumental one.

With that in mind, we got an army of people involved: US Embassy architects to start designing the academy buildings, the vice president and some of his people to identify possible sites for the training center, Colombian security team members to help brainstorm what the academy needed, and so on.

The search for the right site for the academy continued at length.

We saw no less than ten possible locations, but Tom and I soon realized that we were part of an international tug of war that was more than we could navigate. What worked for the State Department didn't work for Colombia, and vice versa. Some locations were too far out of Bogotá, and the embassy wanted the training academy within reasonable driving distance from the embassy. Others were being seized as part of a narco case but were not yet officially owned by the Colombians. We could not build an academy on a potential site. A few otherwise ideal locations had terrain that ended up being not conducive to construction. The vice president, who was in charge of the Colombian side of the project, would say to us, "Listen, we have this great property." But then the embassy would come back and say that it didn't fit their specifications. Eventually, we came out of a meeting with the vice president, and I realized that we had seen every single viable property the Colombians had to offer. When we got back to the embassy, the RSO said to us, "Listen, timing is everything. Maybe we're pushing too huge of a transition right now." Maybe.

Since we had already all agreed that the Colombians were in crucial need of a broad range of protection training, but a new physical site didn't seem to be in the cards, we decided to create a protection academy without the new, cutting-edge training center. We were graciously offered a fantastic facility owned by the Department of Administrative Security, which they used to train their own people, and we happily accepted. The Department of Administrative Security was an agency similar to our FBI, and, for the most part, the training site had everything we needed.

It took about a year after our training program was established for me to get that itch again—like I needed to move on, to look for my next challenge. However, I promised myself that I wouldn't leave the country until every last member of the MOD's protection team— about fifty people—had been trained.

On my way to the academy now, I headed down to the parking garage—we had traded in our embassy driver and vehicle for an armored SUV about six months earlier. My apartment had the nicest, and the safest, garage, so it had become the usual spot for parking the team vehicle.

From there, I loaded the car with my ballistic vest that had been custom-made for my body measurements, a 9mm weapon in a waist pack for easy access while driving, plenty of extra ammunition, my cell phone, and a radio. Although the route had become commonplace for me, I'll admit that every day when I pulled out of that garage, I took a deep breath as I pulled onto the main street, as it was a bottleneck, or what we call in the field a "choke point."

Not long before, my colleagues and I had been called into a special briefing at the embassy. It was held upstairs, which meant we were in "the cone of silence," otherwise known as CIA territory. There was a bit of an awkward silence before the meeting started, people giving looks to each other without saying anything. What the hell was going on? As it turns out, my team members and I had had bounties placed on our heads. The guerrillas had declared war on and placed bounties on any American who was assisting President Uribe's administration—especially those training his people and helping keep the leadership alive. I never shared that little nugget of information with my parents. That would not have been wise.

So, as we sped down the roads of Bogotá, my head tended to swivel quite a bit as I surveyed for potential threats. I picked up Tom, first, then headed for Dave's place. Ah, Dave.

Once we'd ascertained the Department of Administrative Security facility was perfect for the training we wanted to do, we had needed to hire a director of training. Once again, Tom and I had been given discretion to hire the individual we thought most capable for the position. Without any hesitation, Tom and I smiled at each other and at the same time said, "Dave." He was a great instructor, a blast to work with, and had participated in training all five groups of Colombians in the ATA program back in Albuquerque.

When everyone was in the car, we flew down the highway to the training academy. There's a saying that goes, "In speed, there is safety." In Bogotá, I lived by that motto because it had gotten me through perilous situations not just in my protection career, but also in life. The world is difficult and dangerous, and to survive and thrive, you've got to be prepared to deal with curveballs swiftly and with a clear head. Never let them see you sweat, remember? You can't get waylaid by the bullshit, whether that's bureaucracy or chauvinism or a grenade attack. You've just got to keep moving to your next destination.

EPILOGUE

When I first set out to write this book, I planned on writing my entire professional story, which would have also included many of the investigations I have been involved in since my time as a US Secret Service Agent. However, I ended up writing so many pages about my years as a protection agent that *The Protector* became its own book. The various gaps in time in this book are mostly filled by those investigations. Perhaps one day I will complete the story and share those incredible adventures.

In 2000, I was told, not asked, by John Rochon, the Chairman of the Board of Mary Kay Cosmetics, that I would be speaking at the legendary Mary Kay annual Seminar. The Mary Kay Ash Foundation was expanding its mission to include Violence Against Women and John wanted me involved in the launch.

Being hugely supportive of my recently earned master's degree in Forensic Psychology and my specialization in Stalking, John told me I would be giving FIFTEEN one-hour presentations; essentially, the same presentation, fifteen times, over the three-week Seminar period. I laughed and told him, "Thanks, John, but maybe next year. I just graduated and need more time to be comfortable with public speaking and the knowledge you want me to share." Without hesitating, John said, "No. You are going to speak this year," and walked away. I just stood there, dumbstruck.

In my protection career, I had been trained to use many different weapons and to execute high-speed maneuvers in vehicles. I had sized up generals and drugged-up thugs on the street. I had been undercover, interrogated by Internal Affairs, and sold for a couple (well, a lot) of cows. And yet, before, during, and after every single one of those fifteen speeches on violence against women (stalking, domestic violence, and rape), I was not at all comfortable. Frankly, I was uncomfortable being the center of attention, the overt "expert," the conveyor of such heavy information. Nor was I super comfortable with the many women that came up to me after the talks, some crying, all thanking me for my talk and telling me how helpful it was. I was far more comfortable being in my usual role of protector, which kept me in the shadows.

After the Mary Kay Seminar was over, several letters came in to the Mary Kay HQ about the talk I gave. One in particular I will never forget. It was from the daughter of a woman who had attended one of my talks during Seminar. The letter stated how I had "saved her mother's life" and, as a result, their family. She went on to say that for years, after this woman's father left, her mother thought that it was her fault, blamed herself, and essentially stopped living in the present. After attending my presentation, her mother realized she had been a victim of domestic abuse and that her husband leaving wasn't her fault. Since then, the daughter shared, her mother had been happy and started to live again.

Several months later, I was giving a similar talk for the Mary Kay Ash Foundation in Pittsburgh. Two women walked up to me, clearly mother and daughter. It was them—the woman who had attended my talk and the daughter who'd written the letter on behalf of her family. To say a few tears were shed is an understatement. This was pivotal for me. It was a moment in time that I realized, regardless of how comfortable or uncomfortable I was speaking in public, being the expert, or imparting information, I had something to say that people, especially women, needed to hear.

In 2005 when I decided to leave Colombia, it wasn't the end of my career in protection, exactly. It was a change, though, and I felt a pull, something I'd felt since before Albuquerque and way before the State Department mission in Colombia, something I'd felt since that night in Pittsburgh.

My mother was glad when I ended up buying a home in San Diego in 2005, and I'm sure she breathed a sigh of relief when I took a position as COO—an executive!—of a security and investigations firm based in Colorado. During this time, I also worked as a contractor doing Security Needs Assessments for the US State Department's Anti-terrorism Assistance Program in Jordan, Palestine, Argentina, Mozambique, Libya, Bangladesh, and Paraguay. As a Subject Matter Expert (SME), I identified the strengths, weaknesses, and deficits in the respective areas I was assessing and then determined the equipment and/or training needs of the host country in order to enhance the respective antiterrorism "critical capabilities."

In late 2006, I met Mike Janke, and we merged lives in early 2008 in a beautiful home in Bucks County, Pennsylvania. It was here where I got married and pursued a doctorate in Clinical Psychology at Widener University, a five-year endeavor. My father passed away during my last year of the doctoral program. This was particularly sad for me because my father valued education so much and he was not able to see me graduate to become the only doctor in our family, at least thus far.

Lois and Larry Wilkas

After graduation, Mike and I moved to Connecticut where I completed a postdoctoral fellowship in a child- and family-oriented group practice, the Southfield Center for Development. Two years after my father passed, my amazing mother passed away, leaving my six siblings and I to maintain the tight bonds for which my mother was largely responsible. So far, we are doing a pretty good job.

The Wilkas sisters

Two years ago, in 2017, we moved to the Washington, DC, area, where I began to teach Adult Psychopathology at the University of Maryland. After one semester, I moved over to the George Washington University, where I currently teach Abnormal Psychology and my dream course, the Psychology of Crime and Violence. I also currently consult in the areas of clinical psychology, forensic psychology, and various areas of security.

ACKNOWLEDGMENTS

Most of the important endeavors I have pursued in my life would not have been accomplished without a string of people that have helped me along the way. This book is no exception.

My editors, Lindsey and Sal—the dynamic duo. Where to begin . . . For your infinite patience and continued guidance, from beginning to end. For your ability to take my written story and verbal descriptions and magically bring life to them on paper. And for your steadfast commitment to me and this project. The day I signed on with you, I was finally able to exhale.

Maren, for pushing me for so many years to write my story and then trudging through the first version of the book and making so much sense of it. Thank you for understanding.

Tony, for nearly more than two decades of inspiration, encouragement, and support. You have been a mentor, a friend, and a human being I truly admire.

Sue Ann, for introducing me to my editors. And for your courage as a pathfinder, as one of the first five female Secret Service agents. You are part of history that opened the door for me.

Sherri, who, despite my avoidance of your requests to let you read the various drafts of my book, like your friendship, did not relent. Your input was invaluable and pushed me to believe in my work.

And Anna, whose spiritual guidance and insistence finally pushed me to sit down and write my story.

ABOUT THE AUTHOR

Mary Beth Wilkas Janke has more than twenty-five years of psychology, security, and investigative experience. As a psychologist, Dr. Wilkas Janke has worked with individuals who are experiencing anxiety, depression, adjustment challenges, trauma, women's issues, and substance abuse. Dr. Wilkas Janke has also conducted research and published work in the areas of stalking and domestic violence, self-esteem and young women, and stress management.

Dr. Wilkas Janke earned a doctorate in Clinical Psychology after an illustrious and varied career that included being a Special Agent in the Washington Field Office of the United States Secret Service. She went on to become a protection agent on numerous government contracts and was the only female to ever officially protect a foreign president outside of the United States. As part of The Investigative Group, Inc., a global leader in investigative intelligence in Washington, DC, Dr. Wilkas Janke led an inquiry during the "Iraqgate" investigation and an investigation for *60 Minutes* on the Duke lacrosse scandal. She also served as a counselor in the Stalking Unit of Victim Services in Queens, New York, during which time she researched and created a Stalking Risk Assessment Prototype.

Dr. Wilkas Janke holds a doctoral degree in Clinical Psychology from Widener University in Philadelphia and a master's degree in Forensic Psychology from John Jay College of Criminal Justice in New York. She received her bachelor of science in Criminal Justice from Indiana University in Bloomington along with a minor degree in Spanish Language, following intensive studies at the Universidad de Sevilla.

Dr. Wilkas Janke currently works as a consultant in the fields of forensic and clinical psychology and continues to consult in the areas of threat assessment and protective security. She is the Director of Special Projects for Hunter Global Security Strategies, an international security and investigative firm. Additionally, she teaches Abnormal Psychology and the Psychology of Crime and Violence at the George Washington University in Washington, DC.

You can find her online at marybethwilkas.com.

Made in United States
North Haven, CT
24 January 2024